SOUTH BOSTON BOY

A City Boy's Life at Mid-Century

By Joseph Doolin

Roger Morrison + Mary Valentine Dennis Doolin + Hannah O'Neill

Maggie Morrison	+	John Joseph Doolin
1872-1940	1899	1872-1946

Dennis F.	1902-1970
John J.	1904-1964
Joseph P. **	1907-1967
Roger M.	1909-1969
Margaret A.	1911-1973
Anna M.	1913-2006

Thomas Fahy + Mary Melody Michele Pelose + Annunziata Balestra

Delia Fahy	+	Giovan Battista Pelosi
1879-1964		1879-1948

Zita M. Pelose**	1908-1989
John F. Pelose	1910-1996
Oliver J. Pelose	1911-1978
Madeline V. Pelose	1919-1976

Zita M. Pelose** + Joseph P. Doolin**

Joseph
Eleanor
Kathleen

for

Maggie Morrison, the Grandmother I never knew.

South Boston Boy, first edition October 2011.

Published by Bumps River Press.
ISBN 9781463737870

Cover photo: Dorchester Avenue at 9th Street with St. Augustine's steeple and Gavin School in background.

Broadway near Dorchester Street, South Boston. circa 1920.

Chapter One

Making her way homeward from the yellow-brick school building, Anna kicked up little volleys of fallen leaves on the sidewalks to vent her feelings. The nine-year-old was not at all happy that her sister didn't wait for her after school. It was not that she didn't know the few blocks home; it was just that she didn't like to have to pass by the fresh boys on the corner, outside the store. They often had something nasty to say.

Oh, good, she said to herself as she noticed that there was no one on the corner today.

Then as soon as she turned onto her street, Anna looked up from the leaves at all the commotion.

Both a paddy wagon and a police car were in the middle of the street in front of her house, while a huge fire truck was just leaving its space at the curb. Neighbors were out in the street talking to each other in subdued voices and looking up at her front door. The wise guys from the corner were there too. She saw one of them nudging another and pointing at her at the end of the street.

She didn't react, didn't move. Anna just stood there, transfixed, leaning against the Grabauski's house, the back of her head a few shingles beneath their front window. She wanted to go to her own house, but her feet felt like they were sidewalk bricks.

Suddenly her front door opened.

She could see the back of a policeman with no hat on. He was walking backwards, carrying something. Then she could see a second hatless cop, slowly walking toward the other policeman. Something was between them. They were carrying a chair with something on it.

Every time I heard my Aunt Anna tell this story about that afternoon in 1922, she stops here in shock at what happened to her mother, my paternal grandmother.

Maggie Morrison Doolin's thick, wavy chestnut hair was unmistakable. From a half a block away, Anna saw her mother sitting upright on the chair as the policemen carried her down the few stairs to the street. Her arms were tied back to her sides. With dishcloths, it looked. Her face was glowing red. Anna could no longer see her for the crowd, but she could hear her mother yelling at the policemen, telling them to Stop, Put me down, Let me go.

Anna could smell charred wood. She couldn't see any smoke, but the acrid smell assaulted the little girl's nostrils.

Then, her sister Margaret was coming out behind her mother. Mrs. Donovan from next door came out next.

My aunt stood there on that long ago day, watching as the tipping point in her childhood transpired like a scene from a scary picture show with no piano.

Her mother's protests grew louder as the two men, with a third helping from the middle, lifted their ends of the chair up and into the back of the shiny black paddy wagon.

Margaret jumped up and disappeared into the cavity after her, but Mrs. Donovan and the third policeman, who had put his hat on, brought her out to the sidewalk. Anna watched from her vantage point across the way as her sister stood sobbing, "Momma."

Then the back doors of the vehicle were slammed shut. Two of the policemen got in the front, the third went to the police car, where two other officers sat waiting. The one beside the driver gestured toward Mrs. Donovan, who quickly went to the side of the car. In conversation with him, she in turn motioned to Margaret, who joined them. After a few minutes the police car started up and both vehicles slowly made their way out of the narrow city street.

One of the fresh kids went over and said something to Margaret, who looked across the street at her sister for the first time. Margaret and Mrs. Donovan went over to get her. Once back at the front door of their house, the two sisters began weeping in unison, while Mrs. Donovan draped one consoling arm around each child.

Between sobs, Anna could only ask, Where are they taking Momma? Why? What did she do, Margaret? Why are they taking her away in the paddy wagon! Why?

Come into my house, now, and I'll make us a cup of tea, Mrs. Donovan urged, not ready to respond to the little girl's queries, but prescribing her generic remedy. Your father won't be home for some time now, and I don't want you girls going into that house alone. Your brothers will have to help clean it up first. Here, Anna, take my handkerchief, your nose is dripping down to your chin. Help your little sister, Margaret, let's get out of this cold before we all get a chill.

Mrs. Donovan leading the way, they all three stumbled the few feet into her little flat on the first floor of the house right beside the doorway that had just emitted Margaret Morrison, strapped to a chair, hysterical.

Normally, Anna liked going into the Donovan house. It was always clean and orderly, and smelled good. Mrs. Donovan seemed to bake something good just about every day. Even the clothes drying on the back of the big black kitchen stove were neatly arranged.

There, now, Mrs. Donovan said as she poured the girls' tea in matching crockery mugs. We need lots of milk too, don't we? And how about some of that soda bread? Should be cool enough to eat by now.

Margaret, why did those policemen take Momma away in the paddy wagon? Anna asked, not dissuaded by food and drink.

Okay, Anna, interjected Mrs. Donovan, Okay. Your Momma's going to be just okay. Don't fret your head about it. She's just tired, that's all. And, she had another accident up in her kitchen.

When I got home from school, Margaret said, there was smoke all over the house. Especially in the back pantry. I guess Momma was trying to put it out, 'cause she was standing there, waving her apron at it. Waving and waving. But, you know how she gets.

Sometimes she calms down, but not this time. And the pantry was on fire. So, I ran to get Mrs. Donovan, Margaret said through her tea and soda bread. She began to weep again.

Margaret, now quiet, your mother wouldn't want to see you like this, Mrs. Donovan said.. She'll be back home for supper, for sure, you'll see. Now, did you girls see all those sparrows in the school yard this morning? That's a sure sign of spring.

Anna Doolin Butler a dozen years later.

Anna's youngest brother Mikey came home just after the early twilight fell. He had gone to play ball in the streets right after school and was oblivious to the time.

Johnnie and my father Joe-Joe, both teenagers, came in together.

Pa always got home by six. Dennis, the oldest, was working on an ice truck, and he was always late. So, it was Johnnie who went to police station with Pa, while Joe-Joe, Margaret, and Mikey set about the task of cleaning up the house after the fire and its residue.

What have you done with my Maggie? Where is she? I must see her now, my grandfather boomed. A strapping man with bushy hair and a handlebar mustache, he strode into the police station in the midst of the busy neighborhood.

The desk sergeant immediately recognized John Doolin and came out from behind his cage to talk to him. Once John had calmed down, they both sat on a bench, with young Johnnie at his father's side.

All I can tell you, my friend, is what the report says. And that is that Margaret set fire to the pantry behind the kitchen and was fanning it with her apron when her neighbor, Mrs. Donovan came in to see what was going on. When she couldn't put it out herself, Mrs. Donovan sent little Margaret down to the call box to report it and to wait for the truck to come. By the time the men got upstairs, the fire had pretty much spent itself. But, the missus was in pretty bad shape. Beating her arms up and down, grabbing the firemen, hollering crazy things. There was just no way to quiet her, according to the men on the scene.

Now, John, as a friend, I ask you, has this kind of thing ever happened before? Setting a fire in the house is a very serious thing, you know. We're not all back in Galway, y'know, with the big hearths in the middle of the room. This is the city, boyo. The sergeant put his arm on John's big shoulder, and continued, Now, the firemen tell us that this is not the first time she has set fire to the house, John. Is this true?

There have been accidents, John admitted.

Well, look, John, this is a very crowded neighborhood. Especially that part of West Fifth Street where all the houses are small and jammed up together. The sergeant noticed that someone had come in and was standing near his cage for attention. I'm sorry to tell you that we just have to hold her here awhile for observation. The Deputy Chief has ordered a doctor for her tomorrow.

What on earth are you talking about? My Maggie doesn't need a doctor. She's as healthy as a horse.

Confident and glib for his fifteen years, Johnnie asked, My Pa is right. What kind of doctor did the Chief send for, anyway?

A doctor who specializes in this kind of thing. The sergeant never looked at the boy. Now, I don't want to get ahead of myself here, John, but the doc is probably going to send your missus to the place out in Mattapan. For tests, you know.

What place in Mattapan is that?

Have you never heard of Boston State Hospital?

The insane asylum? Johnnie blurted out.

A nut house, you mean? John couldn't believe his ears.

Maybe they can help her, John.

Never thought of my Maggie as insane, he muttered, head down.

Mrs. Donovan was wrong. Maggie did not come home for supper that night.

Boston State Hospital at Mattapan.

Chapter Two

They drifted into a decision, the way so many families do. John never quite understood what it was that the people at the hospital could do for his wife of twenty-two years, the woman who had given him six children, and had been in childbirth eight times.

Sure, she could be odd at times, he told them, but never sick a day in her life – not counting the pregnancies, of course. But, she's a good woman and we need her at home.

He never thought she would be there long. Overnight, perhaps. Then when she didn't come right home, maybe a day or two for tests.

What was he going to tell the men at the railroad where he worked? Don't have to worry about the boys in the pub, he thought to himself, thank the Lord. That closed in January because of the Prohibition. Is he supposed to say that his wife was in a nut house? What kind of thing is that? One thing he was sure, it would never happen back in the old country. He never heard of such a thing there. At least in Cork County where he spent all his sixteen years before getting the boat to Boston. Who knows, though, maybe they had a nut house in Dublin.

At first, Mrs. Donovan helped out a lot. She'd get the suppers for seven people started, and ten-year old Margaret would take over when she went next door to do the same for her own brood of six. Joe-Joe usually got the hot cereal started in the morning. Margaret could brew a pot of tea, and in a few days learned how to make Pa's fried egg.

Johnnie kept the kerosene from running out so the front room wouldn't get too cold for Pa when he came home from work, and Joe-Joe kept the kitchen stove alive with coal. He already knew how to pick it up over by the railway yard.

As Maggie's absence went into its third week, Mrs. Donovan was able to do less. The one thing she made sure she did, however, was to take Margaret shopping at least once a week. Margaret, in turn, began to depend on Anna. Given the 29 months between them, sharing the same bed, and a finite amount of girls' clothes, the two sisters were naturally close. The departure of their mother, and the ensuing responsibilities thrust upon them, brought them closer still.

They could often be seen trudging out to the stores on Broadway, pencilled list in hand, small amounts of money hidden in each of their mittens, Margaret carrying her mother's black oil-cloth shopping bag – her badge of womanhood.

Thirteen-year-old Joe-Joe would be enlisted to accompany them on many such shopping expeditions, not only to ward off the wise guys -- which he was good at -- but also to provide a semi-adult presence in dealing with the shopkeepers, and, of course, to help carry the groceries back. The three were becoming a unit within the family, a unit that shared looking out for younger brother Mikey, and getting food money from Pa and Dennis.

Like most couples, John and Maggie had developed patterns of living over their years together. Coming from different parts of Ireland – she from Middleton town, he from out in the farmland of Cork -- they both arrived in Boston as the nineteenth century was winding down. They met in the rooming house on Grenville Place where they both lived in Bay Village.

From the second week that John got off the boat at East Boston Pier, he worked six days a week for the Boston and Albany Railroad. He got to the yards before six in the morning, and left twelve hours later. He often had to work even later, but sometimes on Saturday they knocked off at three in the afternoon. Never missed a day. He kept that job until they retired him with a gold watch from E. B. Horn.

Maggie came to America to work as a domestic. After losing several jobs in private homes, the happy-go-lucky village girl found herself working in Boston hotels and restaurants. Sometimes in the kitchen, sometimes serving food in the dining rooms. She was well liked by customers and co-workers, but nevertheless, had periods of unemployment. At 27 and just a year younger than John, but well beyond the prime marrying age for the time, Maggie didn't think long about his proposal. He was a steady man, known for not parting with his money. Like herself, he was fond of his beer, but not a heavy drinker.

For more than ten years after their marriage in the fall of 1899 they lived in tenements within walking distance of the railway yards. The farmer's mentality programmed into John's gene code pushed him into wanting a place of his own at a time in which most immigrants were happy with renting. He thought he could do better than two rooms and a kitchen for his wife and four children. Lacking formal education, he went to his parish priest for help in navigating the shoals of property acquisition in the Yankee world of Boston.

Except for $200, which was financed as a mortgage, John paid cash for a tiny row house at 214 West Fifth Street – less than a fifteen minute walk from the railway yards.
It was enough for them. They had two rooms and a kitchen on the second floor, with an unfinished space upstairs under the dormer roof for the children to sleep, which meant that John could be a landlord and rent the small flat on the ground floor. The tenant could pay off his mortgage. The house had one toilet in the basement. No bath.

While life had sunk into a routine after Maggie's departure, it didn't feel normal to her family. Never the most domestic of women, Maggie struggled to keep up with the basics of household management. What she lacked in zeal for home economics, however, she made up in support for her children. Being in this country without family, and not one to make friends of neighbors, Maggie related to her children as chums and confidants. Her removal from the family meant not only operational roles to be filled, but more importantly it meant that they were now a motherless tribe.

Someone else could wash the clothes, someone else could prepare the food, someone else could keep the stoves going, but no one else could provide a mother's love, or the love of a wife. And when the stove did go out, and the house was cold throughout, it became a paradigm of a mother's love extinguished.

John and the children never decided they could do without Maggie, they just did the best they could to keep things going while she was gone.

The first time that John went to visit Maggie at Mattapan, Johnnie went with him. It was a Sunday. After the nine o'clock mass, they got the trolley on Dorchester Street to Andrew Station. Then they took a train to the end of the line at Ashmont and took another trolley to that line's extremity. From there they walked to the gates of huge red-brick Boston State Hospital for the Insane. They looked at the gate, they looked at each other.

When they got inside it was over the noon hour, and the patients were at lunch. They waited in a large, pale green room with windows taller than a schoolroom, high ceilings and plain white columns. The guard called it the day room. There were several other family groups also waiting for lunch to be over. Johnnie was wishing they brought sandwiches with them. John was begrudging the start of the Great Experiment -- Prohibition. Another thing that wouldn't happen in the old country, he thought to himself.

Well, now, hello there, Maggie, John said to his wife as he hugged her when two matrons brought her out.

Hi, there, Ma. How're you feeling today? asked Johnnie. Her famous red hair was unkempt and she was very pale. She was wearing some kind of shift John didn't recognize. Most unusual, her mood. She didn't say a thing to her husband or her son. Just came into the room, sat down and stared.

Feeling any better, there, Maggie? John tried again.

Their attempts at engaging her in conversation were met initially with silence, then monosyllabic responses, and an occasional grunt.

Father looked at son as if the younger male had the answers to the enigma of the woman that was his mother.

After a while, shifting in her seat, she rose slightly and released gas. Maggie had the attitude of a person completely alone.

Have they been giving you enough to eat? John asked, fishing for some way to connect with his wife. The dull stare continued.

What time do they put you to bed, Ma? Johnnie tried. He got nothing either.

When it came time to leave, John reached out his hand to put over hers as he leaned in to kiss her cheek. While she did not respond, he believed that she was aware of his touch, that she knew who he was. Johnnie gave his mother a farewell hug, noting that she smelled funny.

After the two matrons had removed Maggie from the day room, and John and his son were exiting, they were approached by a doctor. Youngish, tall and reedy with light hair and tortoise-framed spectacles, he introduced himself as Dr. Shore.

When can my wife come home, Doctor? John went right to the point. Home is where she belongs.

Playing with a stethoscope over his white coat, Dr. Shore reasoned with John that there was no way his wife could return home in her current condition. The principle of involuntary commitment was explained, while John nodded.

It was dark when they got back home to find the stove out, the house cold.

I never my paternal grandmother. I knew that my father, his father, and his brothers and sisters were protective and embarassed about Maggie's status. They all loved Maggie, and went to visit her every Sunday, and at Christmas as well as her birthday. But it was confusing. As hard as they all tried, it didn't seem like Ma there in that place. She wasn't dead. There was no wake. No funeral. No closure, just the ongoing grayness of life without a loved one who had somehow left them.

And they did not know why.

My grandmother didn't come home for supper that night in April 1922. Nor did she come home for the six thousand six hundred and sixty-five nights she had left to live.

Joe-Joe, Zita, and me, 1939

Chapter Three

Don't knock my family, Zita. Yours moved around so often because your father didn't pay the rent. That's what *Roxbury* people do. said Joe-Joe to his wife every time their arguments turned to the question of whose family was worse.

After all, Joe-Joe was South Boston and grew up in the house that his father owned. Never mind that that was a tiny row house in the Lower End with one toilet -- no bath or shower -- in the dirt basement for the two large families who lived there. It was his house, Grandpa's house. Actually, it turns out that Grandpa and Grandma had at least three prior addresses before the house on West Fifth Street, so they moved around a fair amount as well.

My paternal grandfather John Joseph Doolin left a hardscrabble farm in Cork to come to America. His older brother came over first. Dennis worked on the ship to earn his freight, and when he arrived, he saved enough to send for John to come. John did the same for his younger brother, Roger. None could read nor write. Coming through Immigration in East Boston, the native officers didn't hear the same surname through the brogue of the new-coming brothers, their arrival separated by years. John came through with his name intact, eponymous with the town on the West Coast of Ireland, Doolin, now known as a center for Irish music. Dennis before him and Roger after him came through with the more Anglicized version, Dolan.

Years later when asked about this, and pressed to indicate which was the correct version of the family name, John insisted that his was. "Yes, I was born with this name, this is the name I took with me when I came to America. Can't speak for Dennis. Maybe he always wanted to be Protestant, anyway."

John grew up on a small subsistence farm in County Cork. He was dazzled by a gal about his own age from Cork city, who lived at the same rooming house in the South End. Maggie Morrison worked as kitchen help in some of the bigger homes in Boston, as well as some hotels. They married in the fall of 1899.

Dennis eventually became Chief of Police in a tiny farming town in Massachusetts called Foxboro. It was filled with Yankees. Roger settled outside Worcester and went back to farming.

Joe-Joe and Zita discover Photomat machine, 1931.

While it was the Potato Famine that shoved so many Irish out of their country in the middle of the 19th century, bread riots in southern Italy began the march of 15 million people out of that area between 1880 and 1920. In Boston at the turn of the 20th century, only about 2% of the foreign born were Italians; twenty years later it was 16%.

The reasons for Italian emigration in this period were more complex than the Irish, however. Sixty percent unemployment in the Naples-Avelino area, several bust years of citrus crops, failure of the Italian wine industry, the eruption of Mount Etna, topped by crushing taxes on everything that poor country people need to survive, were gales at their back. This confluence of forces in Italy – primarily southern Italy -- chased out the same kinds of poor, uneducated but tremendously hard working, landless, peasant families as those streaming out of Ireland.

Three big differences were language, the fact that the Irish got here first, and that most of the Italians being from the South, had a much harder time blending in with the native citizenry – culturally and visually. The Boston Irish looked down on the newly arrived Italians for a number of reasons. Not the least among them was that the Italians tended to place a lower emphasis on their children's education, did not send their children to parochial schools or to religious education, and did not support the Church with the same alacrity as their Irish co-parishioners. Perhaps most offensive of all to the Irish was the Italian's postponement of citizenship and participation in the political process.

Giovan Battista Pelosi never remembered his native town of Paternopoli. He was barely three years old when he was taken from the very top of a mountain on the road from Sorrento to Naples. His father Michele came from the neighboring *comune,* or village, of Fontana Rosa. His mother, Annunziata Balestra, was a member of a family that controlled much of the real estate and stone-cutting industry in Paternopoli. Nevertheless, in 1882 Michele and Anunziata opted to leave behind all they knew, somehow got down the mountain from their beautiful aerie and traveled the nearly thirty miles to Naples to get the boat for America.

For contadini like these, just to make the voyage from their village to the dock was a venture into the unknown. The ship took the little family to the port of Providence, Rhode Island, to be with relatives and gain a foothold in the new world.

Years later, Giovan Battista Pelosi had become John B. Pelos*e*. Immigration changed the family name, substituting the final i with an e, but Providence public schools called Giovann, John. My grandfather came to Boston to look for work. Riding the streetcar, he also found a wife.

Delia Fahy scrimped and saved to pay for her fare from Galway to Boston. She could read and write, and no one told her how her name should be spelled. She was just twenty when she and her sister came to America to work as domestics. Delia worked for a family in Newton, and later left to work for the Waltham Watch Company factory across the river.

On her days off, Delia liked to take the trolley into Boston to see the shops and all the different people.

There was no one in her rural village like the Italian man she met on the streetcar. Dark of hair, olive skin, jet-black eyes, well-dressed and polite, John spoke English as well as she did. Certainly not like all the other Italians she had seen and heard about. This was a time in which Italians and Eastern Europeans were not universally considered white. Perhaps it was because neither John nor Delia had family in Boston to react to their interest in a person so clearly from another tribe. Whatever the reason, interest blossomed into a relationship. They married in 1906, much to the horror of Delia's sister, who refused to be a witness and promptly returned to her parents' farm in Ireland.

Joe-Joe and Zita at Craigville Beach, on Cape Cod, 1932.

The two Johns, Maggie, and Delia were among the hundreds of thousands of people who settled in the closest-in rungs of Boston's neighborhoods at the end of the nineteenth and the turn of the twentieth centuries. While the Boston of the 1890s was not only huge and industrialized as compared to that of the 1790s, it was also much more of a melting pot. The Irish influx in the early part of the 19th century was followed by the arrival of southern Italians, Eastern Europeans including Poles, Lithuanians, Latvians, and Jews. They joined the nativists and the small group of African Americans who had begun to move to Roxbury from the South End.

My mother was born in 1907. Named after her paternal grandmother, Annunziata Madalena Pelose was the first of John and Delia's four children. "Zita," as she was known, had two younger brothers, John and Oliver – who was named after Oliver Wendell Holmes -- and a baby sister, Madeline.

Zita's world in the Roxbury of The Great War and the years following was marked by school, which she loved, and helping at home, which she didn't. The chore she disliked the least was caring for her sister Madeline, 11 years her junior. As a pre-teen, Zita would take Madeline in her stroller to walk around the streets of Roxbury, look at the houses, shop windows, and do what the sisters liked to do best their entire lives, eat. They also went to the branch library because Zita could never get enough to read either.

Her family did move around Roxbury a lot. One estimate was once every two years. They lived in several different sections. Quite often their immediate neighbors, up or downstairs, would be Jewish families. Zita would often be the one to turn on lights on the Sabbath.

John Pelose, Zita's father, worked for the Boston Elevated Railway. He was a "checker." He would report on those conductors who were less than scrupulous in collecting and depositing fares on the streetcars. Being an outsider, an Italian in an Irish mileu, he was expected to be loyal to the company, and not conflicted by clan loyalties. By the time Zita graduated from high school in the mid nineteen-twenties, however, he seems to be underemployed. She effectively became the primary breadwinner in the family when she goes to American Mutual Insurance Company in the Back Bay area. Zita was delighted to have a job, get out of the house, avoid chores, and have more time for her reading and going downtown to movies with her friends.

An attractive dark-haired, brown-eyed girl with a ready smile, Zita was well-liked at work, in spite of the speech impediment that she worked hard to mask with repartee. Most of the boys in her Roxbury neighborhoods did not go to high school, and none of her male fellow students interested her. Passing the age of expected marriage -- 18 –21 --she dated only sporadically, and mostly brothers of her girl friends. By the time she is 25, it is assumed that – as pretty as she may be – she is destined to be one of those old maids who put all their energies into a job.

One summer Sunday she rode the streetcar to the beach in South Boston with two of her girlfriends. There she caught the eye of a lifeguard. It is the depth of the Great Depression. Twenty-five year-old Joe-Joe is an amateur boxer, well-known and popular in his native Southie, but like many young men at that time, not exactly on a clear career path. With a sixth-grade education, and no marketable skills, this temporary job is the best that he could do.

After a four-year courtship, and untold hours on the streetcar, Zita and Joe-Joe were married early in 1936. A brief ceremony was held in the rectory of St. Joseph's Church, Roxbury, followed by a train trip to New York City.

The newlyweds lived in a small apartment in Brighton until it was clear that Zita was going to have me, when they move to Roxbury to be closer to Delia, Zita's mother, so she can care for me while Zita works. Jobs are still scarce and Zita has one, Joe-Joe does not. When he can, he does part-time laborer's work at the Railway Express depot in South Station. By now, Zita's parents are empty-nesters living in a third floor apartment in Haynes Park, off Warren Street.

Joe-Joe sent Zita a telegram – a popular form of communication at that time – to mark the birth of his first child. The wire was sent from Suffolk Downs at 11:33A.M. on June 17, the day after I was born. It was addressed to Mrs. Joseph P. Doolin at Boston City Hospital, and said,

"Congratulations on our new arrival hope you and the baby are well will see you soon. Joe."

The back of the Western Union envelope advertised rates of 25 cents for "your selection of fixed texts; 35 cents for 15 words of your composition." In that my father's lavish display of enthusiasm and affection comprised more than 15 words, it is entirely possible that Joe-Joe saved the dime and went with the fixed text. I never heard how he made out at the races. But, Dad was not the type to pace the waiting-room floor, anyway.

Never one to waste anything – including a trip -- Zita wrote a note to Joe on the back of the telegram and mailed it to him. The note read,

"Dear Joe –

I feel fine. When you come Sunday bring a True Story Magazine, some gum, and a pencil with an eraser. I'm writing this with an eyebrow pencil and it's no good to do crossword puzzles with. Also bring a towel and face cloth, my tooth brush and tooth paste, the bottle of Jergen's Lotion in my suitcase, my box of powder and puff.

I won't need the other things because they want you to wear theirs. Also, bring my wire curlers, they are in the suitcase. I miss you a lot, thanks for the telegram. The Hiertys sent a card.

Zita"

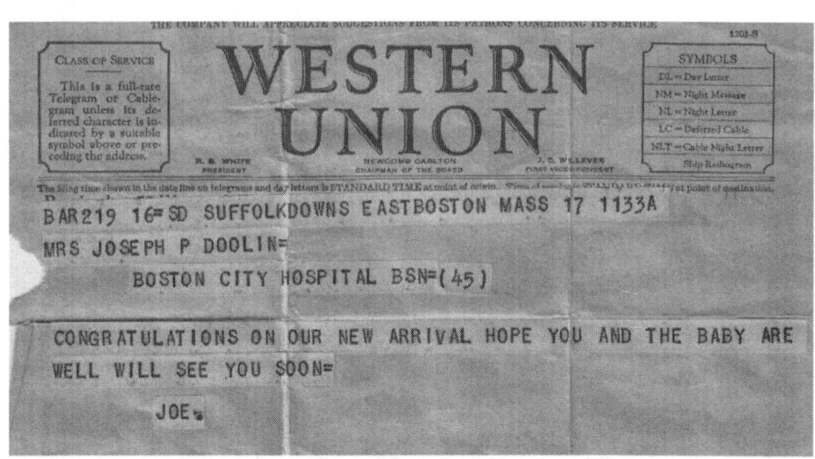

THE COMPANY WILL APPRECIATE SUGGESTIONS FROM ITS PATRONS CONCERNING ITS SERVICE

1201-S

CLASS OF SERVICE
This is a full-rate Telegram or Cablegram unless its deferred character is indicated by a suitable symbol above or preceding the address.

WESTERN UNION

R. B. WHITE, PRESIDENT — NEWCOMB CARLTON, CHAIRMAN OF THE BOARD — J. C. WILLEVER, FIRST VICE-PRESIDENT

SYMBOLS
DL = Day Letter
NM = Night Message
NL = Night Letter
LC = Deferred Cable
NLT = Cable Night Letter
Ship Radiogram

BAR219 16=SD SUFFOLKDOWNS EASTBOSTON MASS 17 1133A

MRS JOSEPH P DOOLIN=

BOSTON CITY HOSPITAL BSN=(45)

CONGRATULATIONS ON OUR NEW ARRIVAL HOPE YOU AND THE BABY ARE WELL WILL SEE YOU SOON=

JOE.

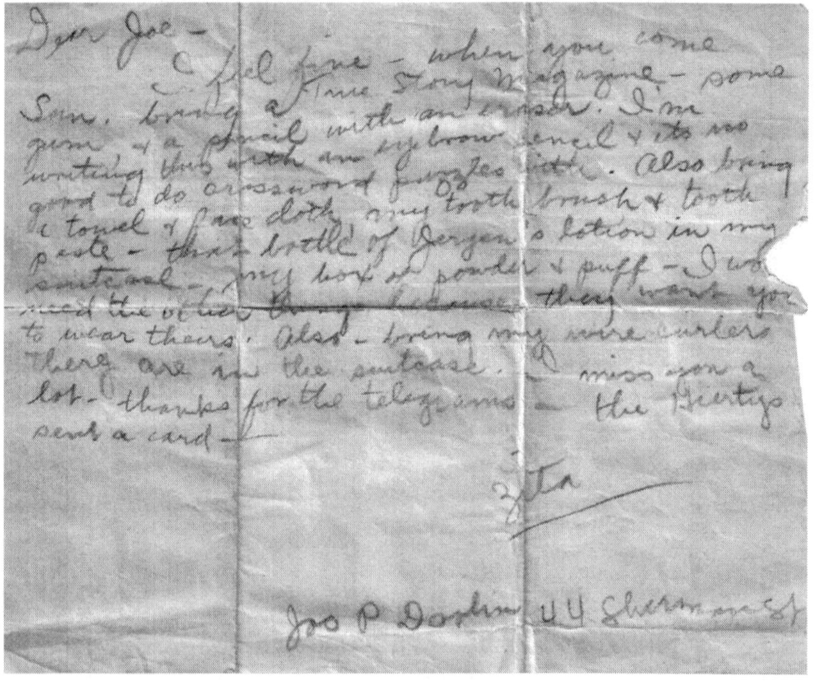

Dear Joe -

I feel fine - when you come
Soon, bring a True Story Magazine - some
gum & a pencil with an eraser. I'm
writing this with an eyebrow pencil & it's no
good to do crossword puzzles with. Also bring
a towel & face cloth, my tooth brush & tooth
paste - that bottle of Jergen's lotion in my
suitcase - my box of powder & puff - I won't
need the other things because they want you
to wear theirs. Also - bring my wire curlers
they are in the suitcase. I miss you a
lot - thanks for the telegrams - the Giertys
sent a card -

Zita

Jos P Doolin U S Sherman SF

The Dudley-Warren area of Roxbury still had the flavor of a streetcar suburb in the early 1940s. Dudley Street was a row of shops and stores. Kimball's Five and Dime, Kennedy's Butter and Egg store had competition from Morgan's, whose vanilla ice cream was in a class of its own. The Sunrise Delicatessen was cheek by jowl with the Warren movie house. Zita and Joe-Joe went to St. Joseph's Church, which had a ceiling resembling the night sky with painted stars marching across. There their son was baptized and there I went to the parish school until the end of second grade, when I made First Communion in a white airman's suit -- a concession not only to the war effort, but also my burgeoning plumpness -- complete with cap.

We lived on the first floor of a generous two-family house at 44 Sherman Street. The back yard was leafy and in parts overgrown with weed-trees, the kind that, when stripped of its leaves, the branches made whips that little boys liked to play with. While neither the landlord nor the landlady -- both Nova Scotians -- were ever seen puttering outdoors, somehow there were neat foundation plantings, including some cabbage-like leaves that I would eat uncooked, unwashed -- while turning up my nose at the cooked spinach on Mickey Mouse plates indoors.

It was not until I started school that I thought much about being different from the other kids. After early September I realized that I was. Rather than being out playing the rough and tumble street games enjoyed by young boys, I seemed to spend all my time indoors with Grandmother.

By this time Delia was housebound, having what was probably an untreated hip ailment that allowed her to walk only with great discomfort. In that Zita worked regularly, and Joe-Joe patched together a week of different shifts, Zita would be the one to drop me off at Nana's in the early morning, and pick me up late afternoon. Not only did Nana live on a third floor, but she was also a very fearful person. There was no way she was going to let a child out of that house until Zita came to get him. Attending kindergarten was out of the question, due to the logistics of retrieving me in the middle of the day. Once I started first grade, Zita had made arrangements with a French Canadian neighbor girl, Alice, to walk me from school to Delia's house. Alice was a big girl. She was in the fifth grade.

Since my birthday came in June, the yard at Sherman Street was a great place for a party. One year, several playmates and school chums came for games and birthday cake. One of the most prized gifts that year was a glass lantern filled with candy. I was notorious for being a finicky eater, but candy I liked.

Nana's "house" was a flat in a wooden tenement building, among several built around a courtyard, or open space off a main streetcar line. There was colored glass in the double doors downstairs and in the windows on the hallway landings. It was very different from Grandpa Doolin's house. Nana 's house was a horizontal apartment with central heating and a full bathroom.

My memories of Nana's house are clearer, more abundant than of my own house in Roxbury, perhaps because I spent more waking hours at her house than at my own. Other than "picture memories," the only memories I have of the interior of our house at 44 Sherman Street, are of playing under the kitchen table and praying in the bedroom with Zita.

Not regularly, but when she was distraught about something, Zita would take her son into her bedroom. We would kneel at the side of the bed and pray together, the mother teaching her child. Her eyes would be focused on a wedding gift which hung over the bed: a crucifix of simple black wood with silver corpus. Most often the prayers had to do with having enough money to make it through the week. Perhaps the answer to one of her prayers was the local politician who came to the house with a chicken. Perhaps. At this stage of her culinary development, a whole fowl may have been for Zita an example of the adage, be careful what you wish for.

Nana's house had radiators in just about every room. The living room was stiff and foreboding. There was a front bay window hung with dark drapes over lace curtains over dark green shades that were usually pulled down half-way in the day time. Opposite the window was a double doorway hung with heavy velvet portieres separating the living room from the next, intended as a sitting room but used as Grandpa's bedroom. Nana slept in a much smaller room at the end of the hall, closest to the bathroom and kitchen.

There was a large, heavy, oval table of dark wood in the middle of the living room with a tapestry cloth and a lamp on it. In later years, when I came on Saturdays to help Nana, Grandpa would leave a dime and quarter under the cloth. Ten cents for the round-trip trolley fare, twenty-five for me.

Other furniture in the living room included a few upholstered chairs and a wind-up Victrola with vertical velvet sleeves, each filled with a 78 rpm disc. Caruso was there, as well as other Italian artists. When I got to be in the second grade, I was allowed to crank up the machine as Grandpa had showed me, and carefully lay the brittle spheres on the velvet turntable. I was transported when I heard the far off voices like imprisoned crickets, and marveled at the magic of technology.

The living room was where my grandfather was laid out when he died. There were still many home wakes then, with big purple sprays on the doors. Since Delia was an invalid, it made sense not to traipse her over the three flights of stairs, plus the outside steps, to and from the afternoon viewing, and again for the evening, two days in a row, as was the custom.

A child's understanding of science is a curious thing. I believed that the brown plastic Crosley table radio on my parents' living room table was filled with miniature people just waiting for the knob to be turned on, lighting up the dial, for them to come to life and entertain the assembled family. Geography was equally mystical: my understanding was that we humans lived on the *inside* of the spherical object called the Globe.

The only radio in Zita's parents' house was built into Grandpa's desk in the dining room. It was a roll-top in dark wood with a lot of pigeonholes on either side of the radio, behind its cloth frontispiece. The tubes could be seen glowing at the back of the radio, perhaps so that the little people could read their sheet music.

Also in the dining room, at the window overlooking the rear passage between tenements, was a sill-high wicker plant stand holding a few plants, probably geraniums without blooms.

Perhaps to remind them of the outdoors – the views from the flat were uniformly of other buildings essentially the same – the living room walls were adorned with a pair of framed colored prints of two elaborate gardens that would seem appropriate for a grand English country house. Each pictured horticultural exercise was a layered affair with tall plants at the rear, shorter ones at front, all harmoniously in bloom in communion with some invisible sun.

The ersatz mantle in the living room – there was no fireplace – had pictures of sons John and Oliver in uniform, a picture of daughter Madeline in suit and corsage just after her marriage to Eddie Callahan.

Delia's bedroom was a tiny one, with a single bed, dresser, table, washstand, and a heavily padded straight-backed chair. The mirror was crowded with holy cards and little brown photographs. In addition to the crucifix over the bed, there was a religious calendar and a framed picture of the Sacred Heart. Lots of pill bottles, lotions, and linaments were in evidence. The smell was not unlike the perfume department on the first floor of Filene's Department Store Downtown.

The green wallpaper had huge gray cabbage roses. There was one window, and unlike the rest of the house, the green shade was usually up, and there always seemed to be a lot of light in this room. This is where Nana spent her day. When she wasn't in the kitchen, she was in her room. Alone.

Grandpa's bedroom off the living room was cool and dark. Linoleum was curling. The dark-colored wood bedstead was massive in proportions, dwarfing the room. A large black crucifix with a pasty white corpus complete with bleeding wounds hung over the bed. The whole room smelt stale. I don't recall going in there much.

One of the most fascinating things in the house -- after the Victrola and the desk radio -- was kept in the dining room on a shelf over the door. Evidently a salesman had sold it to Nana, because it is hard to imagine Grandpa wanting a Holy Viaticum set. It was neatly designed in a dark wood box with a metal cross on the top in imitation silver. Two hasps kept it shut. When opened, with the top upright it made a mini altar. There was a crucifix in the same silver-colored metal, a pair of candles for the stationary holders, cruets for wine and water, little jars for the sacred oils for the last rite, some cotton to wipe off the excess, some cloth towelettes, and other accoutrements of the sacrament of Extreme Unction. The inside of the case was lined with a purple velvet that would have made Elvis swoon. To me, it was like having a little church in a box. Sometimes Delia let me open it and play with the components.

There were two windows in Delia's kitchen. Except in the summertime, one of them held a wooden box to keep butter, eggs, and milk cool enough between the times when the iceman cometh.

It was a miracle how food got into this kitchen. Delia had long been unable to go out to shop. It was still years before her grandson came back as a schoolboy to do housework and errands. Grandpa might occasionally bring home delicacies from the North End, but he was not a shopper. Milkmen delivered to the door then, that's probably how milk, eggs, and butter got there. But someone else was bringing in the bread, Uneeda Biscuits, Royal Lunch – and of course, the canned goods and the ketchup.

The little gas range and oven always seemed to smell, and always needed a match. Delia's oven might just as well have been welded shut. She boiled everything. Everything.

Grandpa was very fussy about his food. He obviously gave up on Delia 's ability to master anything more Italian than "max," boiled spaghetti coated with butter. Defensively, he would use ketchup on everything that his wife boiled. One time he was so anxious to get the bottle started, that he hit the bottom with such force that it splattered the ceiling. Routinely, he would spend major holidays in Providence with his sister, who could cook Italian food, leaving his wife and family in Roxbury.

Maybe this is what started the rumors about his having a mistress. He was also rabidly anti-clerical, having sympathies with the Anarchist movement, and had some connection with either Sacco or Venzetti, Zita could never remember which. He was married in church, buried from church, but like many Italian men of that generation, wasn't seen going, in between.

Delia, Dukie, and Joey, at Nana Day Care 1940.

My cousins Frannie and Theresa – children of my father's eldest brother Dennis-- beat me arriving here on this earth. I was next. Then about three years later, cousin Jackie was born to my father's brother Johnnie – the one who was exiled to Chicago -- followed by Helen Ann to his brother Mikey, whose real name was Roger. However, in the scheme of things, it wasn't hard to figure out that my father was the favorite of The Aunts. Anna and Margaret were yet unmarried and living at home to take care of Grandpa. When I came along as Joe-Joe's first – and a boy -- they were primed to spoil.

Although Zita's baby sister Madeline had beat Zita to the altar, I was also the first grandchild on my mother's side. A few years after Zita's firstborn came into the world, sister Madeline had a daughter, than another a few years after that. So, I was king of the roost on that side, too. Zita's brother John didn't marry until after the War; his sons John Michael and Kevin were much younger. Brother Oliver married after the war as well, but had no progeny.

While there was no specific memory of going to Delia's house before I was in Nana daycare, there is a recollection of the grandparents there as two distinct, warm, loving presences.

Different from going to Grandpa Doolin's house, which was something I did frequently as a young child. The house in South Boston was smaller and more coarsely furnished, but brighter and more lively. With three adults to pay attention to me. Grandpa and Aunts Anna and Margaret. There was no Grandma there. I never met her. She was never talked about. Many, many years passed before I knew that she had been institutionalized at age 51 until she died eighteen years later.

The tiny house on West Fifth Street was obviously built as a single row house as an improvement over the more congested multi-family tenements. It had long been used as a two-family. My earliest memories peopled it with Uncle Dennis, Aunt Betty, Cousins Franny and Theresa on the first floor, all sharing the one toilet in the basement with Grandpa, Anna, and Margaret upstairs. There was no bath. That happened up Broadway at the Municipal Building.

There was no Holy Viaticum kit, either. But they did have something almost as good. In the dugout, dirt-floor basement on the way to the toilet, Cousin Franny had a ham radio studio about the size of a photograph kiosk. It had all kinds of tubes and aerials. As much as I loved playing with it, I was never sure Franny appreciated my interest in it. Among the disadvantages of being an only child for the first five years of life, seems to have been an almost equivalent lack of sensitivity to the need to share, and the wisdom of staying away from older and bigger guys' things.

No radiators anywhere. A kerosene stove in the front room and a big black coal stove in the kitchen just about did it for heat. No central heat. No heat in the rooms at garret level upstairs. When my father and his sisters and brothers were little and their bedrooms were upstairs, they would leave the connecting kitchen door open to let the heat travel up and the kids would run up quickly and get under the covers.

The front room had a console radio cathedral complete with gothic arches and tapestry front, Grandpa's chair, and some others. There was a picture of a nocturnal landscape with the moon shining over a lake prominently displayed. The aunts would give me a mirror and I would try to make the moon shine by reflected sunlight. I would also amuse myself for what seemed to be hours by taking every pot and pan out of the pantry, dragging them into the front room, and banging them together. Grandpa would sit beaming, with his large white handlebar mustache, a bottle of Boston Light Beer near his foot. Boston Light as in lighthouse, not light beer.

When asked about Grandma 's whereabouts, he would say that she went to New York. Comparable then to saying she went to the moon shining over that printed lake. But that was rare. No one ever talked about her. It was as if she had died when she was carried out of the house decades before. Her death eighteen years later did nothing to heal or to close the pain and disfunction triggered by her institutionalization. Like an avalanche, Maggie's illness disrupted her own and succeeding generations.

Pelose family circa 1913: Zita, John, Grandpa, Oliver, Delia. Madeline is yet to be born.

Chapter Four

For Zita's father, life was one ebullient adventure after another. Not a tall man, he was southern Italian contadini-sturdily built, with a balding pate – denying the meaning of his name in Italian: the hairy one. He had light olive-toned skin, warm brown eyes, and wore rimless glasses which he often cleaned after huffing on them in his open mouth to fog them up. It was hard to tell if his grandson was more fascinated by this or by their clamshell case, which snapped in such a decisive way.

Always in shirt and tie, he removed his jacket only in his own home.

Like most immigrants in that period, he never drove or owned an automobile, nor did he own real estate. Once he left Providence for Boston, except for holiday visits to partake of his sister's Italian home cooking, he lived separate from his few remaining family members in this country. He married outside of his ethnic group, and lived in mixed neighborhoods, rather than those with concentrations of Italians or Irish. Of his four children, all graduated high school just in time for the Great Depression; the older of his two sons went on to Boston University. Both sons served in the Army for the duration of the Second World War, one with distinction as a lieutenant colonel in the European theater, the other an infantryman in the Pacific. Three of his children eventually owned their own homes (Oliver's came through his wife's inheritance), and none married an Italian.

Grandpa Pelose's views on societal institutions were very different from those held by Nana. She was a pious Catholic who deeply regretted her later-year inability to get out to the sacraments. He was a cultural Catholic who was a stranger to the church interior, and distrustful of her politics. She was disinterested in politics, he was identified with milder versions of Italian socialism, and perhaps fringes of the turn-of-the century Anarchist movement. She offered up all her sufferings for the salvation of the Holy Souls in Purgatory, his most frequently dispensed philosophy was "You only go this once, enjoy yourself, do all you can, there is no return trip."

Like Joyce's Leopold Bloom, my grandfather was a man somewhat detached from his milieu. He loved going out and about on the town, but was not a part of society. Born in another land, another century, another tongue, he engaged in his environment enough to survive, but was never truly a part of it. With the emergence of Irish Boston in the early twentieth century, Giovann Pelosi, renamed John Pelose, was still the Other.

At a time in which the tribe he represented was not among those populating the transportation system's employment rolls, John Pelose's primary job before was that of a streetcar "spotter." He was checking on the trolley operators behavior, including of course their handling of the myriad nickles and dimes collected, and whether or not some passengers were allowed to ride free. And, whether there was any pattern shared by those who did ride free.

Most of my time spent with Grandpa was while in Nana daycare, but once bonded, we got together later as well. These were the travelling years. Just grandfather and grandson. Nana couldn't go anywhere, being virtually an invalid. And, there was also the sense that she was not quite as adventurous as was he. Even an excursion on public transportation – his only option -- was an adventure with Grandpa.

One trip, which happened just about perennially in the immediate Post-War years, was the trip to the Hotel Statler Christmas party.

In his laer years – he was only 69 when he died in 1948 -- Grandpa worked as a timekeeper in the old Hotel Statler, now Park Plaza, on Arlington Street in Park Square. For his grandson, coming from the sameness of the housing project world, where he would come to get me, to the opulence, size, and complexity of a major hotel, was nothing less than a fantasy trip, the Disney Land of its day. Abutting the Back Bay and steps from Boston Common, the hotel held an elaborate Christmas party for its staff. In addition to Santa, there was also a magician and a comedy routine among the live acts. Statler's kitchen put out an array of special foods as a glittering buffet accentuated by glistening ice sculptures.

Then there were the gifts. Ice skates, roller skates, were among the more than token gifts coded for girls and for boys -- and wrapped. Which was a novelty, because Santa always ran out of gift-wrap when he came to our house.

Grandpa introduced me to all his co-workers, including the hotel manager, making a Sister school boy feel very, very special and almost grown up. In retrospect, the coded message here was something like, Here is my blond-haired, American" grandson. I'm really one of you after all.

I was also impressed with my first visit to the North End. Having grown up in Providence, and gravitated to Boston's North End only in his late teens and twenties, Grandpa conveyed his appreciation for its visual and gastronomic delights with all the gusto of a religious pilgrim. After getting off at the Haymarket stop, he would head through the open-air market, greeting and haggling with selected vendors as he shopped en route to Hanover Street.

What I experienced there as a boy was more like a big outdoor party than a market. No canned goods in sight. No cashier's station, no counter where men pulled items down from high shelves with long poles. Just food, food of all kinds, even things that hardly looked like food, all arrayed in pushcarts, bins, and tables with rims to keep things from falling off. Whole fish gawked at me with their eyes and mouths open. Slabs of animal flesh, carcasses of lamb, fowl and what looked like large rodents but in reality were rabbits, hung from racks. Pyramids of tomatoes, eggplant, squash gave off aromas so different from those at the South Boston market on Broadway.

Then we went to a store on Hanover Street that only sold cheese. Wow, the smells in there, I thought. Nothing like the

Velveeta we have at home. Over on Salem Street there were sweets stores and bakeries. Finally, Grandpa decided it was time for lunch. The European Restaurant on lower Hanover had not yet taken over the block and at that time occupied only one storefront. The booths along the walls had velvet curtains that could be drawn for dining privacy; the menu was in Italian. I thought that my grandfather forgot how to speak English, because once inside the European, except for a few words to me, he spoke only in his native language.

Those few words included Have you ever eaten octopus? as the waiter brought plates to the table. Also on the table and new to the kid from Southie were ravioli, tripe, and stuffed artichokes. We finished everything.

Another time we went to the North End to do some shopping for some relatives of Grandpa's who couldn't get out. When finished, we got back on the El – as the Boston Elevated Railway was known -- and went to Columbia Station, just over the Dorchester line from South Boston where we started out. From there it was a healthy walk on the Mile Road to an area known as Columbia Point, site of a massive public dump.

Before the Columbia Point Housing Project, before the Veteran's Housing that preceded it, the Quonset huts were originally built to house Italian prisoners of war. During the World War II years more than 50,000 Italian POWs were secretly interned in U.S. camps. There were 7000 in Massachusetts – Deer Island, Peddocks Island, and Columbia Point. After Mussolini fell in 1943, Italian-Americans could visit these camps to bring food and supplies to friends and relatives.

Grandpa had heard that one of his relatives was being held in the Columbia Point camp. We arrived at the gate to the camp, shopping bundles in arms. Before stating his business,

Grandpa introduced me to the guard as his "American grandson who lives just over there," gesturing to the Dorchester Heights Monument in the distance. "My grandson, he's a South Boston boy." When he thought this had sunk in, he proceeded to inquire about his relative, and was given a pass to enter. Either the South Boston boy looked sufficiently American, or kids didn't need passes. At any rate, I trotted in behind Grandpa.

The half-oil can shaped houses made from corrugated steel were all lined up in rows making a fascinating little city, complete with commissary and chapel. There was some barbed wire in evidence, and a few U.S. soldiers around, but otherwise the feeling of the place was like a Boy Scouts' camporee. The men lolling around outside their quarters, some poking at little gardens, hardly resembled the devils who were booed and hissed at during the Movietone Newsreels. We found Grandpa's relative in one of the dormitories way at the end of the camp. Seeing us approach, a wizened middle-aged man came out of his tin house and stared at us as directly as a bear coming out of the woods. Once recognition took hold, then embrace and kisses, followed by jabbering in Italian – for what seemed like a long time.

They went inside to a room where two men were sitting at a simple wooden table. Over a single gas jet, Grandpa and another man proceeded to make a splendid luncheon for five. On the way home the old man explained to the child the difference between visiting and just dropping off food. "It would be good for them just to have a taste of home, but even in war, even in a prison camp, it is more important to act like family."

When we got back to the Old Colony, Grandpa was just beginning to tell Zita about our day.

We went shopping in the North End, and then brought some food to . . .

The door opened, Hello, how are you? said his son-in-law.

Hi Joe, said his wife. Pa is just telling me about what he and Joey did today. Go ahead, Pa.

I was just saying that we went to get some food in the North End to bring to a sick friend over in Dorchester. We had lunch there. About two o'clock. That's it. The boy has a good appetite.

Undoubtedly, at another time, outside earshot of her husband, Grandpa told his daughter the rest of the story. It is doubtful that Joe-Joe would have been enthusiastic about his son and heir visiting an Italian prisoner of war camp.

Dorchester Heights, Thomas Park, South Boston.

Easter Sunday 1950, Old Colony. In matching hats, Kathleen and Eleanor are on either side of Zita. Note presence of grass as well as absence of cars.

Chapter Five

We won the war, We won the war, We won the war, over and over we chanted sitting along the little picket fence opposite the entrance of our building, churning small American flags.

The excitement in the warm May afternoon air was palpable.

School had let out early. Students in countless classrooms across the country that Tuesday morning heard President Truman announce the unconditional surrender of Germany. That was followed by special radio programming all day long. None of the usual shows were on until almost supper time. Winston Churchill gave a speech. Eleanor Roosevelt talked about her late husband. Archbishop Spellman from New York said a prayer. There were interviews with people on the streets of cities all over the world. And, there were no sponsor's messages.

We had followed the war through newspaper headlines, radio accounts, and movie theater newsreels. Everyone had a relative overseas in the service. V-Mail personalized the connection with the boys over there. At eight and nine years of age, we knew the meaning of the star in the field of white bordered by red- and-blue rectangles hanging in so many windows around town. And, we knew – but perhaps did not fully understand – the difference when the blue star turned to gold.

We were aware that it had only been in the past year -- since D-Day last June -- that the war's outcome seemed to be turning in our country's favor. Lately, people were talking about Hitler, and wondering of his whereabouts. Just a few weeks ago he seemed to have disappeared. Some said he was hiding in South America.

But, today, that was all forgotten in the communal celebration that was V-E Day 1945. How great it was to be alive and living in that place at that historic time.

This community in which we lived was both an accidental one, and a quite natural one.

It was a village of a neighborhood within an old Northeast seaport city of considerable size. For us kids waving flags along the still raw wooden fence, our everyday world was bounded by a far narrower reality: the few blocks between home, school, church, and the handful of shops in between. The place was new -- less than three years old. The brown tile floors in every apartment had yet to accumulate the uneven yellowing terrain of self-polishing Beacon wax that built up in later years. Outside, saplings and tiny shrubs spoke of hope. Benches and playground equipment were intact and allowed to do their jobs. Graffiti had yet to be named, but there was plenty of room for hopscotch art on the new pavement.

As is often the case with new housing developments, this one, called Old Colony Village, was seen by neighbors in the surrounding older structures as a desirable place to live. It was new. New at a time at which virtually all civilian products were shelved in favor of the War effort. Not only did these housing units constitute a significant relief to the severe pre-War need for safe and sanitary housing for city families – a need exacerbated in the war years when defense workers flocked into the city -- but they also featured state-of-the art plumbing and appliances. At a time and in a place in which refrigeration and central heating were novelties, indoor toilets were often shared by more than one family, and most households in the neighborhood depended on the municipal bath-houses, each apartment in the new development had a new kitchen equipped with gas stove and refrigerator, and its own full, three-piece bathroom, supplied with continuous hot and cold water. All this in a unit heated by clean steam heat requiring no fetching coal, wood, or kerosene.

We never thought of ourselves as poor. The poor were those displaced persons in Europe, the little kids in Africa who got the pennies we put in Little Black Sambo's basket, causing him to nod his head in thanks. Not us kids in the Old Colony. Not these families. We were middle class. When questions were asked about where we stood in our country's pecking order, we were told, "Just about average." Right in the middle. Everyone else lives pretty much the way we do. Sure, there are really rich people who live far away, and have parties on yachts like the movie stars, but most people in the U.S. are pretty much like us.

With the swoop of a moving truck, my life had changed.

Zita was no longer working – Joe-Joe got a job working for the City -- and number one son was no longer in his grandmother's care, didn't have to spend all his free time at her house, indoors. We moved in summertime, between my second and third grades.

With my old neighborhood and school far behind me in Roxbury, I had no idea what lay ahead for me in the new land of South Boston. To ease the transition, my father and Uncle Mike gave a hard sell on the quality of the ball fields and beaches of my new town, with Uncle Mikey stressing the added advantage of Joe's Spa and the Bay State Ice Cream parlor. For me, it took a while to figure out that in this new place, I got to go outdoors -- on my own. A whole new world!

It was exhilarating to have so many kids around. I even got to play with other boys my own age. Playing outside for what seemed hours and hours was pure heaven on earth. Didn't have to leave home and there were enough boys to play cowboys with, enough boys and girls to have really full group games on summer nights after supper.

As a child I seemed to have had an active interior life. Organized games and sports came later, but in those early years it was cowboys and Indians, followed by the inevitable movie re-enactments that kept my imagination percolating. There was a movie almost always going on in my mind, with which I was engaged interactively. Stories I told myself lived in the theater of the mind, while those I saw on the movie screen were acted out physically. Sometimes alone, more often with other kids. A fantasy world of palaces, armies, and an imperial family was conjured up, featuring a boy emperor greatly resembling the storyteller.

This boyhood capacity to amuse myself for what seemed to be hours, going over imagined buildings, rooms, conversations, costumes, also had a physical, real-world component. Fallen leaves became golden mountains rising from the street gutters, mountains that I would kick, wallow in, and strew in all directions. Snowbanks became forts and castles on the sidewalks. Some had windows, and platforms from which to defend the icy realm.

After about age eight or nine, however, sagas from Hollywood begin to compete with those I created. So, I began to re-enact movie themes at home.

To do so properly, of course, I had to have the right get-up. Thanks to Aunt Anna and Margaret's largess – about which you'll hear more in a later chapter -- I had the requisite outfits to play cowboys, and to play Indians if I chose to go to that side. Ever the sucker for the underdog, I guess I often did, much to horror of my little friends. For other settings, I would improvise.

Apparently I was intrigued by movies set in ancient Greece and Rome. They were always having battles and giving speeches draped in the same yard goods like the statues in church. Absent a wardrobe mistress, I had to make it up as I went along. Bath towels approximated the look of togas, with one minor problem. They never stayed in place. Naturally, Zita thought her son was very creative, and lent him some common pins.

I wish I had pictures of this plump little kid, draped like Julius Caesar but with his underwear in plain view. As supportive mother Zita was of this kind of game, dad Joe-Joe was not. Which I quickly picked up on. I would try to time my last act and costume shedding to his return from work. Sometimes – apparently too often – I forgot to remove the straight pins from the towels. Since Joe-Joe was usually the first to take a shower, this did little to strengthen father-son relations. Joey, for God's sake, what's going on? I'm clawing myself to death here! I look like the tiger keeper at Franklin Park. These things hurt. No one puts pins in towels. I'm bleeding.

Moving from the apartment in Roxbury to the housing project in South Boston represented the achievement of a set of goals that Zita and Joe-Joe had worked for since their marriage. By this time we were a family of five, my two younger sisters having joined us toward the end of the war years. Getting the City job was the key. Zita no longer had to work, which meant that they did not have to live close to Delia for child care.

It also meant that Joe-Joe could return to his beloved South Boston, where he had a broad social network – both friends and family. A former Golden Gloves Champion and mini-celebrity, my father had a wide circle of friends and admirers. He was also close to his father and his sisters and brothers – all of whom but Uncle John lived in South Boston.
Has mentioned in a preceding chapter, his mother had died. Zita's support system was more geographically diffuse, centering on her friends from work who lived all over the city, and her parents and sister in Roxbury. Her two brothers – unmarried at this time – were both still overseas.

If there was any stigma attached to residency in public housing in the 1940s, it was more that the developments tended to be located away from the social and commercial core of their neighborhoods, than any economic or class branding. World War II was still raging, housing was scarce, and the Depression mentality still pervaded the lives of the urban working poor.

An apartment was an apartment. A new one, that was both affordable and with state-of-the art kitchen and bath, was a rare find.

Neighbor Nancy (Purdy) Welby and her grandmother.

My family came to the Old Colony Village development when it was only a couple of years old, and still had little picket fences and marigolds around the walkways, grass lawns, trees, and ample play equipment for children. Our first apartment was just across the street from a public school that also had a playground. Blocks of three-story red-brick buildings were built around a rear courtyard housing a chain-link fenced-in clothes-drying yard, a large paved playing area ideal for stickball and other games, such as "Cigarettes," "Red Rover," "Relieve-O," among others, and an incinerator at one end. All trash was disposed here, and periodically the maintenance man would light a fire to burn it. When the wind blew the wrong way the newly dried clothes were bespeckled with ashen remnants of neighbors' trash.

Old Colony with picket fences in place, mid-1940s. Kathleen and Eleanor are enjoying the front yard at Old Colony.

Early developments like the Old Harbor and the Old Colony were considered to be progressive solutions to the social issues of the first part of the twentieth century, which centered on sanitation and housing availability for what would now be described as lower middle class, two-parent families. It was not until the 1960s that awareness of the deficits of large-scale public housing grew. Initially, applications for an apartment in the Old Colony required that a family must have resided in Boston for at least a year before their application, they must have been living in "substandard conditions detrimental to health, safety and morals." The family income could not be more than six times the apartment rent.

And, all families were treated the same. Everything in the project was uniform. All apartment floors were brown asbestos tile with black borders, all walls were painted yellow. There were no closet doors, just rods to hang curtains over the stored clothing and other items. Bathrooms were brand-new three-piecers: sink toilet, tub. Kitchens had the latest stoves and refrigerators. Each building was accessed by a set of concrete stairs from street level leading to a wooden door with glass panes above the handle. There was a key to this door, usually held by a first-floor family, but no one then felt unsafe enough to use it. The hallways were covered with yellow ceramic-tile bricks, floors were concrete. When my family first moved in, families took turns washing the hallway floors and sweeping the stairs. Far different from the situation when we moved out.

I don't remember much about the layout of the first flat we had on Burke Street, where we stayed just over a year, but the apartment on East Ninth is very clear in memory. From the street, up the half dozen stairs that was to become the staging for the assembled neighbors as Greek chorus, in the front door, past the line of metal mail boxes on the right, and a hard left and there we were. The metal door opened directly onto the living room, which was one open space with the kitchen, with a cabinet as partial screen. A nine by twelve linoleum wouldn't leave much of the floor showing. Living room windows were less than a yard from the exterior front door, providing for excellent monitoring of the other eleven families' coming and goings – and of course a front mezzanine seat for the conversations out on the stairs.

Being girls, and little ones at that, my sisters got the smallest room. (I am still hearing about that.) Their window had the same view of the front as the living room, but my room had a bonus, besides its size. From the window, if you looked past the building across the way, down East Ninth Street, your eye could take you almost to the ball fields out on Columbia Road. The only obstruction was another building on Mercer Street, but that had a pedestrian archway, a cut-out in the building to allow people to walk from the projects out to the fields and the beach beyond. My card-table desk was up against the window, and untold hours of daydreaming took me down the street, through the keyhole, and out to the open sky of the parks and Carson Beach.

My parent's bedroom and the bath room were on the other side of the "house," which was quieter and had views of the clothes drying yard, the back play area, and the incinerator – all of which were accessed by a cement-covered path the width of a sidewalk.

The back walkways to the courtyard were enough of an incline to propel a sled in winter, and for downhill roller-skating the rest of the year. This was where pre-teen kids got their first taste of gravity-based outdoor sports. Our kitchen window happened to face on such a walkway. One afternoon when I was studying in the kitchen – closer to the food supply than my room on the other side of the building -- a lone little girl was skating down the incline. Steel wheels connecting to hard concrete made a piercing cry, again and again, as the little girl trudged up the hill and then coasted down.

After being distracted several times from my rote memorization of history homework, I decided to invoke the greatest power of that time and place. Positioning myself out of sight, just behind the kitchen curtains, and conjuring up the most stentorian voice I could, Mary Muldoon...this is . . . God speaking to you, little Mary stopped in her tracks, mid-slope, God, do you hear? Assured of her attention I continued, October is the month of the Holy Rosary. This, Mary Muldoon, is the month of October. Now is the time for you to pray. Now. Right this minute! Mary Muldoon's head was perpendicular to the concrete pavement, eyes squinting at the fall sky. Go, I tell you, go into the house and pray the rosary. Do not come out again until tomorrow. Do you understand me? Mary Muldoon?

Pre-First Communion soul Mary Muldoon sat down on the concrete walk, fumbled with her skate key, unstrapped her skates, and ran around to the front door. While there is no way of knowing whether the innocent spent the afternoon in prayer, no one can recall ever seeing – or hearing – her skating on the slope again. Many other sights and sounds happened on that slope over the years, but Mary Muldoon did not return.

Clothes drying area where Mary Muldoon had her religious experience. Sidewalk slopes (right) to back yard.

As the years went on, in an effort to retain her children's babysitter, Mary Muldoon's mother worked very hard to make a romantic match between the children's sitter, Elfreda, and the voice of God behind the curtain. Little Mary's father was a State Police Officer, her mother worked a few waitress shifts a week, and had imported Elfreda from the Dorchester neighborhood where they used to live. For some reason, it was not Wayne from the second floor, or Johnny from the third – both also roughly Elvira's age – who was recruited to be the bait, but me. From the first.

I still can't remember what Mrs. Muldoon offered to get me to do it. Maybe it had something to do with preventing a police investigation of impersonating God. For whatever reason, I felt trapped. The Almighty succumbed to a few "dates" while Elvira was sitting the Muldoon kids up on the third floor. Once all six kiddos were under control, we would sit on the couch and talk about schoolwork and drink cocoa. She made popcorn, and unlike Zita didn't curse like a sailor when she burned a few kernels. But, the electricity just wasn't there. The Supreme Being's interest was probably still preoccupied with the Shannon girl on the first floor. After all, hers was a very religious family.

Group calisthenics at Carson Beach.

The Old Colony was – and is – strategically located in South Boston. It is a short walk to Carson Beach, to the Dorchester Heights, site of a grand white monument to the memory of the British evacuation of Boston on Saint Patrick's Day 1776, and a marvelous area to play "fort." The Heights has spectacular, 360-degree views of downtown Boston, the Blue Hills, and the Atlantic Ocean.

Kathleen poses amid greenery of Old Colony.

The housing project abuts a broad expanse of acres of playing fields and is but a twenty minute walk from Castle Island. Many units have a view of the strandway and the water beyond. From my bedroom on East Ninth Street, I used to think I could see the water. I would look out the window, as far as the eye would go down the street, and across Mercer Street until it stopped at a project building between obstructing the view of Columbia Road beyond. However, there was a pedestrian archway through the building, which reminded me of a keyhole. Through this aperture I thought I could see the playing fields and the water beyond them.

The beaches seemed huge and clean. Carson Beach was less than ten minutes on foot. My buddies and I would take peanut butter sandwiches, a towel, and spend the day. O, the freedom of swimming and playing ball on those endless days of summer without grownups present! Even when our family went to the better beaches of Nantasket and Scitutate, I still preferred Carson Beach. I guess because it was a kid's place.

There is excellent public transportation in South Boston. Two bus lines embroider the town and go to Downtown and to Copley Square. Long gone are the noisy orange streetcars with wooden slatted benches capped by brass handles -- the backs of which could be reversed at the end of a route so they would face forward as it retraced its steps -- that originated at the extremity of City Point, clanged down Broadway and Dorchester Street to the subway at Andrew Square one way, and to Broadway Station the other.

The Old Colony in the 1940s and 1950s was a family development. While the economic condition of project families changed somewhat in the thirteen years my family lived in the project, two-parent families continued to be the modal package. Kenny Coughlin was an anomaly in my circle of friends, because his parents were separated. My father doesn't live with us, was how Kenny put it, awkwardly.

When we moved into the Old Colony Village Development in summer of 1944, it was a decent, wholesome, albeit no-frills place for working poor families to live while they moved up the socio-economic ladder. Fast forward thirteen years, we see that tenant composition had changed noticeably. Teenaged gangs ruled the hallways, which were used both as party palaces and as urinals. Longer-tenured residents found that the newcomers did not share their values around child-rearing, sanitation, noise control, mutual responsibility, and other areas central to a dozen families sharing one building.

The Old Colony was begun in 1939 to relieve the housing shortage in South Boston, and to provide safer, more sanitary family housing. It opened well after Pearl Harbor. Priority was given to applicants whose breadwinner was working in the defense industry, secondarily to police, firemen, and other first responders, and municipal workers. There were no elderly people, virtually no single men out of their upper teens (they were all in the service), and all the adult men worked all day. A few of the women did too.

There were a dozen families in our new building, four to a floor. The O'Tooles, the Shannons, the Grays, and the Doolins were on the first floor. Our living room windows and the O'Tooles flanked the front door, and a part of the stoop -- or in South Boston, the stairs. The Bartons, the Finnegans, the Brusteins, and the Eastmans were on the second; the Moores, the Buckleys, the McGivers, and the Cassidays were on the third. All the men except one-legged Dan McGiver worked.

Neighbor Marge LoCicero O'Malley 1954.

Tom O'Toole was a U.S.Customs officer, Bill Shannon sold insurance, Jim Barton was a bookkeeper at Boston and Taunton Trucking. Jim Finnegan was a steamfitter at Fore River Shipyard, Art Brustein was a clerk somewhere, Vance Eastman worked in a laundry. Mr. Moore worked at the Charlestown Navy Yard. They moved out to buy a house and a State Trooper, Joe Muldoon, his wife and six kids moved in. Bill Buckley worked at the Edison, Jack Cassiday was at Gillette. Dan McGiver worked on the railroad until his accident. It took him a while to hobble up the front steps on crutches, then two full flights to his third floor aerie. The only time he had a problem was coming home after a night at Haley and Maguire's, his and the Missus' favorite watering hole 'way over in Uphams Corner. Then, he was noisy going up the stairs. Something unusual for this building.

Project front stairs where everything happened. Our living room window is to left of door, the O'Toole's to the right.

Ten of the twelve families were Catholic. The Eastmans were Episcopalians, members of Grace Episcopal Church near Andrew Square. The Brusteins were Jewish. In later years, after her husband died, Mrs. Eastman became a Catholic. She had gotten so used to baking cakes for various St. Augustine's fundraisers, and three of her five sons married Catholics, so when Grace Church closed, rather than join St. Matthew and the Redeemer Episcopal Church up in fancier City Point, she crossed the Tiber, became a Catholic, and joined St. Augustine's. She was home spiritually and socially.

The front stairs were the social center of the building. Women gathered there on good afternoons, and just about everyone came out on the hot summer nights. It was an age-integrated phenomenon. While there were always more kids out and around the stairs in the afternoon, it was also common to see them there with the adults in the evening. These gatherings also served as filtering agents for those visiting residents of the building. The most notable occasional visitor was the pastor, Father O'Connor, who would pass the gauntlet of those assembled to call on the one family in the building who never sat out.

The Shannons, along with the Eastmans, and the McGivers, had a four bedroom apartment to accommodate their larger families. The Shannons were on the first floor. Mr. Shannon and my father were the only men in the building who always wore suitcoat and tie to work. The Shannons were very religious. Mrs. Shannon was a daily communicant and read the hours. Two of her three daughters were nuns in cloistered communities, two sons came back from the War and were commuting students at Boston College. The other brother did not go into the military, seemed to have some limitations, and worked everyday as a dishwasher in a downtown hotel.

Michaela, or Mishy, was in the same grade at St. Augustine's as was I– but of course, in the girl's class.

Father O'Connor would usually come for dinner at the Shannon's. This was unusual, because no else in the building ever had anyone – let alone a priest – come for dinner. The only time a priest came to your house was to administer the Last Sacrament. Further evidence that the Shannons were special people. Perhaps that was one reason I was stuck on Mishy.

In addition to the usual boy activities with other kids, I often went to visit relatives on my own. I was exhilarated with a new sense of independence, partly age related, partly a factor of the compactness of the new neighborhood. At first, when I discovered I could find my way to my paternal grandfather's house, a dozen or so blocks away, I would go in the daytime, after school.

It was when I was perhaps eight or nine years old that I did something quite out of character.

One bright fall afternoon I went to visit the Aunts Anna and Margaret, Grandpa having died the previous year. As yet unmarried, they remained in the house. En route I stopped at a weedtree and ripped off a couple of branches and stripped off the leaves to make whips. Exactly like the kind that cowboys used in rodeos, I thought, having just been to one with Joe-Joe at the Boston Garden. One of the acts was Lash LaRue. Lash was a cowboy, usually a "goodie," or a white hat, who fought bad guys with a 12-foot long bullwhip.

Up the narrow stairs to the second floor I went to knock on the Aunts' door. No answer, obviously not home. After waiting a while, just in case, in my Lash LaRue wannabe persona, I went downstairs to inspect the new renovations. No one locked their doors in those days, certainly not in an uninhabited flat.

Uncle Dennis, Aunt Betty, Cousins Franny and Theresa had moved out of the first floor apartment of my grandfather's house to another flat nearby. Possibly so that the family could get a bathroom of their own. Anna and Margaret had had some firemen come and paint and wallpaper in their spare time. Anna was "seeing" a fireman who had recently come back from the Navy overseas. The flat looked great! All the dark woodwork was gone, the whole place – all four rooms – sparkled with light and bright cleanliness.

To this day I cannot explain it, but something took possession of me. Perhaps the opposite force of the voice speaking through the kitchen curtains to Little Mary Muldoon. I grasped the weed-whips tightly, one in each hand, and dipped them in the open cans of paint that had been left on the floor, and proceeded to emulate Lash LaRue. Each of the walls was a bad guy closing in on me. I had no choice. I had to do what Lash had to do: I thrashed and whipped until there was added color and texture covering the new wallpaper. Throughout the living room. I also fought the woodwork, windows, and ceiling. And I won. Messy work, but it had to be done.

Not my fault that some boob left the tops off the paint cans.

Then, satisfied that evil had been held at bay for at least another day, this third-grader sauntered home leisurely for supper after a hard afternoon's work of preserving law and order in the lower end of South Boston.

The Aunts never squealed. But, the next time I went there, they were home.

We have a bone to pick with you, said Margaret.

Now, I had never heard that expression before, so initially, I thought they wanted help in preparing a turkey carcass for soup. Or something like that. However, that was not quite what they had in mind. They explained that after having the apartment downstairs freshly painted and papered for rental to new tenants, someone came in and splattered paint all over. They couldn't rent it like that. The new tenants had to stay where they are, and wait until the Aunts could get the painters to come back. Firemen had to re-schedule their work, come back to Fifth Street to re-do their work. The downstairs living room had to be completely re-papered, the woodwork and ceiling repainted. That was going to cost a great deal of money.

Someone did this, do you know who? asked Anna, screwing up her face.

It could have been done by some of the boys on the street, Margaret said, hoping. You know, we're not going to tell your father, but we just want to know, they said together, almost responsorially.

Trapped. After all these years I am still not sure if I confessed because it was the right, honest thing to do. Lash would have confessed. Or, did I confess because they had me? And, what did I have to lose? After all, it was their fault. They got me started on this playacting business, giving me all those costumes. What did they expect?

Later on when I was a bit older, I also traveled around the neighborhood in the evening. In addition to the "tonic" and cake that were waiting at the relatives, there was another factor: the magnet of a brand new entertainment medium. Television was new in the years just after the War. My parents didn't have one. No one in our building had television then. Even if a family had the money to buy a set, there was the issue of where to put the antenna. In those days, they were all fixed more or less permanently on roofs. Project families had not yet negotiated how they could do that in public housing.

However, on foot I could get to Uncle Mike's to see Milton Berle on Tuesday nights. My father's youngest brother and his wife Helen – who was the daughter of Lithuanian immigrants – lived several short blocks away, just beyond the perimeter of the Old Colony on the top floor of a triple-decker on Vinton Strreet. They had one daughter, several years my junior. Mike worked in the garment district as an inspector for Clippercraft, a manufacturer of men's suits. Aunt Helen loved to shop, and they always had the latest postwar consumer treasure. They were among the first families in South Boston to own a television set.

As successful as his younger brother was, Joe-Joe would often use Mikey as an example in his Depression-child sermons on job selection. "Get something steady, like the City or the Edison. Even if it doesn't pay as much, you know you'll always have a job. My brother Mikey, now, has that big job at Clippercraft. Does well, I'm happy for him. But, he could be laid off tomorrow. Lookit what happened to my brother Johnnie. Faircloth and Gold moved him to Chicago. Chicago! Can you imagine?"

Let the record show that Johnnie was promoted to a better job with more pay and more responsibility. But, it was a thousand miles away from South Boston.

When Aunt Margaret got married, for a nickel bus ride I could get to her and Uncle Dick's up in the really nice part of the neighborhood, City Point, to watch "I Remember Mama" and "Man Against Crime" on Friday nights. Uncle Dick's real name was Cornelius, and no one questioned why he went by

Dick instead – or, for that matter, why Roger was Mike. Dick was production manager for a wholesale house on the Fish Pier.

The Bay View bus stopped across M Street from their house, on Eighth. Ordinarily, the wait wasn't more than ten minutes, even after nine in the evening. One late winter Friday evening, I stood shivering at the stop in the remnants of a snow shower that didn't stick, having had my fill of television shows and cake and tonic, and waiting for the bus to take me back to the project. There were a few other people there too. My nickel was in my mitten. As the bus pulled over to the curb and squished some slush my way, I started to move toward the door, and as I fidgeted with my mitten to get the nickel out, I noticed a wad of paper in the gutter.

Picking it up, I put it in my mitten, thinking it was something to read on the bus, and got on. Once settled, I realized that I had found seven dollars. It seemed like so much money. Not only could I hear Sister Agnes Patrice, but I could *see* her telling me what to do. "Find the owner and give it to them," Sister said. "It doesn't belong to you. Make an honest effort to find who lost it, and give it to them."

Well, the wad was there before we got on the bus, so it doesn't belong to any of the people waiting with me. It must have been dropped by someone getting off the bus, before I came to the stop. With my stop coming up very soon, I moved up to the seat behind the driver and told him of my quandary.

Maybe you can find out who dropped it and give it to them, I asked the operator, proffering the wadded bills.

> Look Sonny, the man said while watching three grown-up people deposit their dimes, I'm not gonna know who dropped that. It's too bad. Really is, but it's their loss. Happens all the time, I'm afraid. Here's whatchado: Take your girl friend out for a banana split and movie with it.

I tried, I thought to myself, *so I won't even mention it to Sister. The bus driver must have known I was too young to have a girl friend to treat.* Besides, even if I did what he jokingly said, I would still have had a small fortune left over. So, I treated my sisters to éclairs from the Argus bakery and kept the rest of the fortune. Any since windfall is always compared to that bonanza. Just to quiet any residue of nun voices in my head, I bought an extra dollar book of chances on the St. Augustine's raffle of the moment.

Blinstrub's Village nightclub on D Street.

The project was surrounded with conveniences. Very few people had autos, domestic refrigeration was still a novelty, and storage of food products in general was limited. People shopped close to home, they shopped often, sometimes daily Stores lined Dorchester Street and East Eighth Street.

While it seemed that every corner had a variety store, Cheever's at East Eighth and Knowlton Streets was the source of seven cent dill pickle treats. Argus Bakery on East Eighth and Mercer Streets had the carbohydrate overdose monopoly in the neighborhood until the donut shop opened. We discovered lust when introduced to Argus's eclairs and neapolitans. Bell's Cash Market (in its corner of Dorchester Street and Eighth iteration) was a good-sized butcher shop that carried some other items as well. Elm Farm Supermarket was a labyrinth of canned goods. Between Bell's and Elm Farm was the five- and ten-cent store. Thankfully, the owners were not as child-suspicious as Slocum's on Little Broadway. The new Doughnut Shop on Dorchester Street near the corner of East Ninth was located sufficiently far enough from Argus not to be competition, even although Argus made superb plain doughnuts, and their jellies, while not exactly round, were equally good. Also on the short block between East Eighth and Dorchester Streets there was a laundromat, a fish store, and a Chinese laundry.

Gallagher's (Tobin's) Drug Store separated from its competition Vale Drug, by a block and a half, had better ice cream. There was a cobbler shop near the bus stop at East Eighth and Dorchester Streets, and a hardware store on Dorchester Street near Old Colony Avenue.

DiNatale's Barber Shop on Dorchester Street midway between East Ninth and Burke Streets was where this project kid with the Irish name heard Metropolitan Opera broadcasts for the first time, and, to the pride of his Italian maternal grandfather, liked them.

A bit farther away, separating the Old Colony from the Old Harbor projects were the Stop and Shop, Bay State Ice Cream parlor, and Sarni Dry Cleaners.

The Doughnut Shop and the Laundromat were both new businesses, opened by returning war veterans. Kids would spend several minutes watching machines in one window turn sacks of flour into gloriously scented fresh doughnuts, and in the next almost as miraculously make clean clothes out of soiled. And, you didn't have to go out back and hang them on the line, if you put them in the dryer that spat them out ready to wear again. Without ashen speckles.

One of the big kids (probably seventeen) upstairs brought all his working uniforms to the laundromat to be washed and dried, then went home to take a nap. Realizing that he left his pay envelope in his pants pocket, and fearful that his money would be like mushed tissue when wet, he ran up the street to the laundromat. Forget something, son? asked the proprietor. Yeah, my week's pay was in my pants. That's all I got. I need to get it out. Stop the machine -- please. Calm down, kid, let me show you something back here. He took the young man to a little back room where he saw a clothes line strung with tens, fives, and ones. One thing I learned in the War overseas is that American currency is more like cloth than paper. Your pay envelope fell out as I was putting your things in the dryer, so I hung it up here to dry. Is it all there?

It was.

Some convieniences came to us in the project. In addition to the rag man with his plaintive chant, and the man buying fat and bartering it for soap, there was also a variety of produce peddlars – all of these vendors plied their trade in horse-pulled wagons. Then the lay-away man driving a sedan with dry goods in the trunk would come through the streets of the Old Colony. The dense concentration of potential customers in the streets of the Old Colony made it a salesman's dream.

In the summer time, what we as kids looked forward to were the precursors of the ice-cream truck: Cuban Coolers and Pony Ice Cream. The former was a dark-skinned mustachioed man pushing a wagon with an umbrella on top, calling out "Get ya Cooban coolers!" For a few cents you got an upside-down dunce cap filled with shaved ice over which he would pour whichever of the many syrups that intrigued you that day: banana, vanilla, strawberry, pineapple. My sister Eleanor was so taken with the little pony pulling the Pony Ice Cream wagon that she wanted one almost more than she wanted the packaged ice cream treats. Later, the call of the Cuban cooler man, and the tinkle of the pony's bell were replaced with the sharp jangle of the ice-cream truck.

The Church was huge then. In the U.S., and especially in the Northeast, this was the era of Triumphalism for the Catholic Church. In the space of a mere century Boston Catholics went from an inconsequential ministry to French, German and Irish immigrants, to become a major force in the civic arena. Their cathedral on Franklin Street burned during the Great Fire of the nineteenth century, but was rebuilt in the speculative South End as a huge puddingstone temple in witness to their importance. Their archbishop was now a cardinal and resided in a splendid Italianate mansion hugging the Newton line in Brighton. Catholics hadn't seized the White House yet, but that was coming.

Most families in the project went to St. Augustine's. That saint's mother, St. Monica, had her own church in Andrew Square. But that was a wooden church. Even the altar was wood. St. Augustine's was red brick like St. Joseph's in Roxbury, but it was much larger. Its altars, both upstairs -- which was the province of the grown-ups -- and downstairs, where the kids went, were of whitest marble. An 1880 expansion of the

Archdiocese's oldest worship space, a mortuary chapel built two blocks away in 1818, St.Augustine's church had a majestic steeple -- depicted in cover photograph -- with a four-sided clock with an illuminated white face that had to be shut off during air raid drills. The rectory on F Street hugged the church building on Dorchester Street that was beside the public junior high school next door. The convent, grade school, and high school (for girls), and the gender-segregated play yards, were behind on E Street.

Perkins Kindergarten Graduation 1950. Kathleen is to the teacher's left.

And there were the bars. They were everywhere. Car stops, bus stops, in the middle of blocks, even up on Broadway. There were bars, there were taps, there were saloons, there were clubs, cafes, there were blind pigs – leftovers from the

Prohibition Era when many pubs were underground. Everywhere, but on the water - - except for Dorgan's Captain's Room. Monsignor Waters of St. Brigid's is credited with saving South Boston's beachfront areas from going the way of Revere Beach. Nonetheless, not more than a dozen years after repeal of the Volstead Act, the rest of the neighborhood was imbedded with public drinking places.

Privacy within the housing project building was, shall we say, somewhat limited? Like the urban villagers they were, everyone in our building knew just about all the salient details of everyone else. Take the Buckleys, third floor, right front. Betty was a very heavy woman; Peter was slight, looking somewhat like a person out of Picasso's blue period.

They often went out drinking with their floor neighbors at the rear right, the one-legged man on crutches and his wife. Betty and Peter had two children, also named Betty and Peter. Peter was the baby, and this is the story of how he was born.

She usually took sponge baths, but one unusually hot August day when she was pregnant with Peter, "Big Betty" -- unfortunately so differentiated from her daughter, "Little Betty" -- decided to take a bath, there being no showers in the project at this time. However, when Big Betty was through, she couldn't get herself out of the tub. She was literally stuck. Her husband wouldn't be home from work for several hours. Little Betty was only seven, and lacking strength sufficient to break the seal of suction and yank her mother out of the tub. Big Betty sent her daughter door-to-door to fetch whatever women were in the building at that time. Only two were not either out shopping or cooling off at Carson Beach. Combined, the two could not budge Big Betty.

After much clucking and some discussion, the group wisdom was to call the police. When Boston's finest in blue arrived, and after a blanket had been modestly, draped over Betty, four grown men crammed into the tiny bathroom. As delicately as possible the quartet pulled and lifted, pried and shifted. Twenty minutes and a loud smacking sound later, male voices were heard to say, There she is, She's up, and Easy now. Big Betty said only three words, but repeatedly: O my God!

The cops quickly retreated to the hallway, to be replaced by the original two building women and three others who had materialized since this tableau began. There was also a stairwell audience of seven stubborn children who had resisted being shooed away. The women helped damp Big Betty into bed while they ransacked her bureau for something to put on her. Over by noon, this episode was relayed throughout the building and those adjacent before three. By five it was a topic of discussion at the Eighth Street Tap, around the corner, by six at the bar up on Dorchester Street, six-thirty at the Car Stop Café on Broadway, and two pubs in Andrew Square simultaneously. When Peter got home at 7:30 he had already heard a version of the story, and was not pleased.

Peter was more upset two months later when his wife went into labor. He was at home the Sunday afternoon her water broke. After running downstairs to use a neighbor's telephone to summon a cab, Peter went back upstairs to assist his wife down the two and a half flights of stairs to the street. Peter could not have weighed more than a third of Betty's displacement, but he loved his wife and valiantly tried to help her downstairs. Because of her size and condition, Betty had not been outside the tiny four-room unit since before her bathtub episode. She hadn't been down the stairs for over a month before that.

They stumbled out the door of their apartment, Betty ever so slowly angling herself sideways through the door jamb like a grand piano. The stairwell was steps from their door. Slowly they went down, Betty leaning on the railing and Peter trying to both prop her up and keep her balanced -- knowing that he faced certain death should she fall downstairs on top of him. Each and every time Betty's foot searched for a new step down she moaned, O my God, with differing intonations and levels of desperation.

Midway down the first flight, Peter yielded to Betty's pressure on his shoulder and fell two steps. Without him, Betty lost her balance and fell over him, landing against the yellow brick-tile wall three steps from the bottom.

'S coming out! Peter, it's coming now! O my God!

Any of the other eleven doors in the building not open at this point, were now. Suddenly mothers were shushing children, shooing them back in their apartments. Fathers became scarce. Ohhhh, Betty Buckley is having her baby in the stairwell, announced Mrs. Eastman, whose door was less than six feet from the distraught woman. Another woman came out with towels, another went back to her house to get some blankets to make a privacy tent of that end of the stairwell. Someone else blocked traffic from the first floor. The neighbor with the telephone called -- who else? – the police. Moans, cries, grunts, Big Betty was not quiet about her travail and everyone knew about it. Including the expanding number of children who had gathered on the lower stairwell.

Peter was a nervous wreck. As much due to the public nature of his embarrassment as the health and welfare of his wife and aborning child. By the time the boys in blue paid their reprise visit to the building, little Peter was born, had been bathed, his cord cut, and was wrapped in towels covered with an overcoat. The cops helped mother and child down the remaining stairs, and the cab having long since gone, took them to hospital.

For children in this building, it was past time to hear about the stork bringing babies, or infants found in cabbage patches. After Big Betty's birthing adventure in the stairwell, all us kids knew exactly where babies came from.

My father had taken to bringing me in town to shop for clothes. Because I was "heavy-set," translate: fat. Back to school and Easter were the big excursions, with an occasional foray for winter gear. We went to Kennedy's on Summer Street near Washington because there was a Husky Shop on the 5th floor, and because Joe-Joe thought they had better quality than the local options. The Kennedy boys' department walls were lined with pictures of local high schools in shots evocative of Ivy League catalogs.

One of Joe-Joe's friends was a successful entrepreneur, "Law" McCabe. Law owned a chain of greengrocery stores. East Broadway, Meetinghouse Hill, Jamaica Plain were among the neighborhoods graced with a Sunshine Fruit Store. I came along with my father sometimes when he would help "Law" trucking fruits and vegetables from Chelsea to his stores, and sometimes in the stores as extra help. One Thanksgiving the McCabes had the Doolins to their new house in City Point for dinner. Perhaps to relieve his guests' house envy, Law talked about the bank owning more of the house than the McCabes. Still a nice house, I thought. So what if a banker lives upstairs?

Although project families then didn't necessarily feel poor, the more time elapsed after the War, the more there was a sense of class consciousness. That winter day walking to school when I felt especially proud to be wearing a brand new coat from Kennedy's -- the Soviet-feeling number of metallic bronze fabric with imitation fur lining and collar, with a belt around the generous waist -- may have impressed me because none of my schoolmates had new coats that year. In thinking that I could be mistaken for a rich man's son, I was beginning to think that that meant someone from outside the projects.

Later on, as a 14-year-old freshman at Cathedral High School, getting on the streetcar outside the project and seeing groups of older guys from City Point en route to Boston Latin School gave me pause. Those guys seemed so – in today's language -- cool. They also seemed rich and self-confident. Probably only a couple of years older than I was at the time, but of normal weight, they seemed like poster boys for the Kennedy's Department Store college-boy look.

Being somewhat familiar with City Point, I was just as aware that they lived in houses as I was that they were wearing seersucker jackets. The jackets could be seen. That they lived in real houses was something I could feel.

Interior Aquarium had 55 fish tanks, one contained a very old sea turtle.

The Aquarium at Marine Park opened on Thanksgiving Day 1912. It was a stucco building with red tile roof topped by a cod weathervane. Frolicking mermaids graced the arched entryway. Despite its popularity with families and children all over the City, due to lack of funds, it closed in 1954 and was later demolished.

Jordan Marsh's "Salute to America" 1951, Washington Street, Boston.

Chapter Six

Both paternal aunts were still single – there was a war on, you know. They worked for Gillette, lived with Grandpa, and obviously had sufficient disposable cash to indulge Joe-Joe's firstborn. Living in South Boston, working just at the Broadway Bridge, it was a treat for them to go to the big stores Downtown to shop.

Beyond the local shops near the project, their town boasted a variety of larger and more varied stores along Broadway. "Big" Broadway shopping encompassed the area from Perkins Square at the intersection of Dorchester Street and East and West Broadway, westward toward Broadway Station until about F through E Streets.

Here was Perkins Supply, a huge hardware store; the South Boston Market, an early superstore featuring aisles of canned goods, a butcher shop, produce section and a row of prepared-food stations including even Chinese food.

South Boston Savings Bank was housed in a Greek temple at the top of a half flight of stairs used for Bond Rallies during the World War II years.

There was a gas station that also did car repairs for the few people in town who operated autos.

In addition to the Post office and beside Woolworth's (there was also a Kresge's) at F Street, was the Broadway Theater, operating seven days with matinee and evening shows, and an extra Saturday morning kids' show at 11.

There was a Waldorf Cafeteria opposite the Car Stop Café, a local barroom located strategically at a streetcar stop near the intersection of Dorchester Street where two carlines crossed. Everytime I eat watermelon I think of that caefteria. When Grandpa Pelose died, my mother went to Roxbury to be with Delia and help with the wake – which was held at home – arrangements.

As was common then, the wake was held at home, in Grandpa Pelose's third floor flat. I recall walking up the stairs to visit Grandma at the wake, and being told that Grandpa would not want me to cry. My sisters had been put in the custody of next door Mrs. O'Toole, and my father took me for a walk. We ended up having a meal at the Waldorf; for dessert I had watermelon, which was served without the rind and diced. That fascinated me, for some reason.

Gorin's Department Store was where your mother went for curtains for the house and underwear for herself. Pobers was the children's clothier. Men got their haberdashery items from the Bay View Hat and Cap Store just outside Perkins Square on Dorchester Street.

Two furniture stores – Ellis and Carey -- faced each other across Broadway at F Street.

The interstices between these community essentials were filled with smaller shops with more focused clientele. Like the place that sold live fowl.

There was another shopping area, "Little" Broadway. Serving the historically more residential area of City Point, this was on East Broadway concentrated from Flood Square, at the intersection of Broadway and I Streets, to L Street.

Reflecting the nature of this neighborhood, shops here were a bit more upscale.
Small dress shops, a religious articles store, a greengrocer (Law McCabe's Sunshine Fruit), a mini department store, were some of the attractions. Two big ones stand out: The Strand Theater, a movie house in competition with the Broadway; and Slocum's

toy store – home of the mother lode of gimp. Gimp was plastic lacing material that came in yards-long strips about a quarter of an inch wide. Originally a camp craft, it became a postwar craze. Kids wove the stuff into keychains, watch fobs, wallets, just about everything. Slocum's had every color imaginable.

The town supported three ice cream parlors. Known for its banana splits, Joe's Spa was the Maxim's of the trio barely on East Broadway at Dorchester Street. Stahl's was smaller but also had homemade candy, and Bay State was newer and more utilitarian in a small strip at the rotary on Old Colony Avenue at Preble Street, between the Old Harbor and Old Colony projects and opposite the ballparks.

From the project most people took the streetcar the few stops up Dorchester Avenue to the corner of Broadway. If they walked, they usually took the streetcar back with their shopping bags. But, definitely, the only way to get up to City Point was to take the streetcar. Sometimes, when going to the Strand, youngsters would walk and spend the two-nickels round trip carfare on candy at the movies. The walk home was inconsequential because we would be engrossed in re-staging the show en route. For project kids, the only draw to Little Broadway was either the Strand or Slocum's. Mr. Slocum, however, had a special antenna to detect kids who came in without money to buy. They were watched very closely.

Perhaps if we were growing up in any ordinary town, we would have been content with the shops we had. But, in that our town was actually a neighborhood of a big city quickly accessible by public transportation, we had something else to explore.

As younger children, trips to Downtown Boston were usually seasonal – Easter and Christmas. After Easter Sunday mass and devouring baskets of candy, and then a big ham dinner at noon, many families – bedecked in their spring finery -- would troop in to one of the nearly two dozen downtown movies palaces, each one larger and more ornate than the next, to sit indoors in the dark to watch Bud Abbot and Lou Costello or Bob Hope and Bing Crosby. This was how we celebrated the Risen Lord.

Usually not beginning until Thanksgiving weekend, the major Downtown stores would unveil their Christmas windows. Families would flock in, small children in tow, to watch the animated dioramas of Santa's workshop, scenes of ice skating in the country, and miniature railroads.

Anna, Joe-Joe, me Eleanor, Kathleen, and Margaret. Note opening in building at end in right.

As I got older, I became more familiar with Downtown Boston. Even as a child, it was clear that the Downtown shopping area trumpeted by the Aunts was a magical place. No more than a dozen or so compact blocks radiating from the intersection of Summer/Winter Streets and Washington Street housed major department stores with ground floors that smelled like perfume factories, a kaleidoscope of smaller specialty stores – milliners, button shops. bookstores, cutlery stores, jewelry shops, separate clothing stores for men and women – the district hummed year 'round.

While most of the stores we gravitated to were closer to the Washington Street side, Tremont Street, parallel to Washington and facing Boston Common had been the home of Boston's more upscale shopper. R.H..Stearns anchored this area and was flanked by scores of dressmakers, leather goods, and other merchants catering to the carriage trade.

The Aunts were very happy with the selections on Washington Street, however. Some of them even featured food. Department stores such as Jordan Marsh and Gilchrists' developed reputations for signature products as adjuncts to their tearooms or restaurants, as a means to draw customers in and keep them coming back. Huge, sugary blueberry muffins spoke to Jordan's Yankee heritage and claim to reflect New England taste. Heavenly macaroons were Gilchrists' way of saying that ethnics were welcome. Both drew lines to purchase and great applause when brought home. Filene's restaurant was very early on a proponent of healthier eating.

Christmas and birthdays were marked by imaginative gifts from the Aunts to pique a little boy's enthusiasm. Costumes were a popular item. Cowboy costumes, Indian outfits, doctor kits, erector sets, all played a special part in my play life. Garbed in the Aunts' gift cowboy suit, I would play for hours under the kitchen table on Sherman Street in Roxbury.

The table was of butterscotch maple, and had two leaves which pulled out from either end of the shorter side to provide additional surface. One of my games was to drape towels over the sides of the table, put on my cowboy outfit, and go into the space under the table, pretending it was a wigwam. As I lie on the floor looking up at the underside of the table, and its metal label pronouncing it from Paine's of Boston, it never occurred to me that I was a cowboy in an Indian house.

The cowboy suit is long gone, but the table is still in use, as is the memory of the Aunts.

Always in a pair, Anna and Margaret came bursting with excitement, bearing their gifts and their gusto for life and for fun. These two women were simply thrilled for any occasion to make someone surprised and happy. Christmas Eve was a time to make the rounds to visit family members. By streetcar, mainly. No one in the family circle had a telephone yet. Cars were out of the question during the war. It was mysterious how they knew who was going to be home and who was going to go out and make the rounds.

The bathroom in the apartment on Sherman Street was just a bathroom, but when my family moved to the then almost brand new Old Colony Housing Project in South Boston, we had state-of-the-art bath appliances for 1944. This included a tub with running water. The Aunts were still living at home with Grandpa, still sharing the one basement toilet with the four downstairs tenants. For baths, they would walk to the municipal building on Broadway, more than a dozen blocks away. So, one afternoon soon after my family was settled into our new project flat, the Aunts came with bags of things of their own – as opposed to presents for someone else. They went into the bathroom and stayed for an interminable time, coming out smelling like talcum powder, and freshly bathed and changed.

As I paced in the hallway with tightly crossed knees, Zita reminded me that it was our turn to do something nice for The Aunts, and – we didn't have to wrorry about their leaving pins in the towels.

R.H. White's Department Store, Washington Street, Downtown Boston.

The war had been a huge black-and-white tapestry looming in the background of my young life. Zita's brother John, the first on both sides of the family to go to college, graduated from Boston University in 1936 and joined the Army reserves as a First Lieutenant, while working at the Watertown Arsenal. In 1941, Uncle John reported for active duty at Camp Polk, Louisiana, where at 32 he became one of the youngest captains there. He was a supply officer serving in Europe for most of my consciousness about the war.

I wondered whatever happened to the magic slate pad that my other maternal uncle, Oliver, an enlisted Army man, sent from somewhere in the Pacific. Sitting on a swing in the Perkins school yard, I was in awe of this complete novelty. Perhaps 5" x7", it was a pad with a black gummy base – not unlike Etch-a-Sketch – with a celluloid cover sheet and a stylus. Writing on the cover sheet could be erased just by lifting it from contact with the base. No one in school, not even the sisters, had ever seen such a marvel. It was all the more fascinating when I was told that it was taken from a captured Japanese soldier on an island so very far away.

Building the morale of the troops was a community project. Church groups, parents, school children all took the responsibility to write, to send Care packages of food, stockings, mufflers, mittens, reading material, and other items from home. Everyone was urged to write to the fighting men and women.

Both Uncle Oliver and Uncle John wrote V-mail letters to Zita. V-mail, or Victory Mail, was a great midcentury innovation. One sheet of paper was both envelope and letter. The serviceman wrote a letter, filled out the address, and turned it in to his superior officer. Officers censored "sensitive" material, forwarded the letter to a process which made a microfilm copy. When officers wrote V-mail, they were expected to censor themselves, which may have explained the terseness of John's communiques. The microfilm copies were then flown to the States where they were printed out and mailed.

The Vmail technique not only saved space on mail planes, but also protected against espionage. My mother kept the V-mail letters from her brothers in a rubber band on a shelf in the living room. When she wrote in response, she would take her letters to the post office to have them copied, reduced, and shipped by air as V-Mail. This process cut the time between mailing and delivery. We can assume that the Post Office was Zita's censor.

Newsreel coverage of the Allied Forces bombing of a big monastery in Italy called Monte Cassino disturbed a lot of people Stateside. Grandpa Pelose was born not far from there. A socialist and anti-clericalist, Giovan was unmoved about the loss of Christian monasticism's founding site; but, he was so agitated about the expected civilian casualties in the town closest to it that he went to the movies twice in one week. Normally, he went once a year. Grandpa wanted to see if he could see his relatives.

Newsreel reports on World War II were as much a part of the midcentury movie-going experience as cartoons and previews between the two feature-length films. Even the Saturday matinee of twin C westerns, obviously packaged for younger audiences, had war coverage through the new medium of cinematic journalism just as consistently as serials. German and Japanese soldiers always looked cruel and not quite human. Their planes and tanks never seemed as good as the American ones. Cheers, jeers, and boos, at the same decibel level as during the other components of the cinematic bill of fare, were aimed at the newsreels at judicious moments too. The French and Italian forces were pictured as informal, ragtag groups of less than enthusiastic soldiers.

There was no question that the newsreel portion of the movie experience was more real than the other items on the bill, but it was also a piece of entertainment, and an opportunity to engage in communal patriotism.

Never mind that the chronological sequence of events depicted in the March of Time, Pathe' News, or Movietone footage lagged behind radio and newspaper reports. Newsreels were essential propaganda instruments -- especially for kids, who rarely read beyond the newspaper headlines and the funnies. Big people read newspapers with care then, but they too relied on newsreels, which were usually repeated daily for a week, along with the feature films. It was no less vital as news packaged as entertainment because the various battles, the factories churning out the armaments, and the movie stars entertaining the troops overseas, all came to life.

Pulling together, pitching in for the war effort had become a part -- an important part -- of everyone's life. It was thrilling to see how eerie the housing project looked without illumination during an air raid drill. Flashlights strobing around blackened village streets. Civilian Patrol dads with white helmets and sashes patrolling the perimeter of the development, enforcing the lights-out requirement. The few autos had the top half of their headlights painted black.

The parish church ran tin-can drives. My job was to cut the other end out and step on them to flatten them so that more could be packed in a smaller space.

My friends and I were especially fascinated with the air war. Decks of cards featuring the different kinds of airplanes, illustrated booklets to aid in sighting enemy aircraft over U.S. skies, and balsa models engaged school-aged boys throughout the war years. Because I spent endless hours scanning the skies for invading planes, I was convinced that I was a part of civilian defense.

Homeland consumption was closely regulated. Ration books were a fact of life. They covered everyday basics such as meat, eggs, butter. Oleomargarine was brand new and didn't count. However, it was sold white, like lard. Later in the war years it came in newfangled plastic bags with a coloring capsule in the bag. As soon as you bought it, you could squeeze the capsule and color the whole bag. But not before, lest it be confused with the real thing.

People with cars had separate ration books for gasoline. No one in my Roxbury world had a car. Moving to South Boston in the summer of 1944, I was aware that some of my father's friends had automobiles.

When Uncle John came home after the war was over, he came via Tennessee where he spent several months demobilizing his men. A Major by this time, he appeared at the door of the Old Colony flat one summer day, like a ghost. Skinny, but alive. He introduced his sister and her family to his new wife, Margaret, until recently a Baptist from Clarksville, Tennessee. Margaret drove to Boston in her Ford Coupe, with John as passenger. Uncle John said that he wanted to take his sister's family out to buy them some new clothes. I rode home in the rumble seat with a brand new blue slack suit with bone buttons.

Uncle John Doolin, exiled to Chicago as sales rep for Faircloth and Gold Curtain Company

Chapter Seven

One event that pushed Joe-Joe to apply for a larger apartment was the Visit.

Bigger than the Aunts taking over the bathroom, was the coming of Uncle John and Aunt Minnie. This was the other Uncle John: my father's older brother banished by job necessity to beyond the pale, Chicago.

The bathroom invasion only lasted an afternoon; the Visit a whole summer.

John was the most upwardly mobile of the Doolin clan. He worked his way up from factory floor to salesman at Faircloth and Gold, and now wore a suit and tie to work. He sold curtains and draperies to department stores. Faircloth and Gold had their Boston headquarters near A Street in the industrial buildings near the wool warehouses.

Like Joe-Joe, Johnnie had a very low classification for the draft due to age and having a child. Early in the War, he was transferred to Chicago. Towards the end of the War he was reassigned to Boston for the summer months only. Something to do with the roll-out of their new postwar line of paper curtains and drapes.

So it came to pass that Uncle John, Aunt Minnie, and Cousin Jack – three years younger than me – came to spend the summer with our family of five in a four-room, two bedroom, one bath, project apartment. Who or how slept where is long forgotten. What is remembered is the pajamas with bows.

A word about the family political dynamic at play here. Joe-Joe was close to his brother John, having bonded not only in helping out in the house when Maggie was institutionalized, but they also took road trips together as young adults, mostly in connection with Johnnie's work as a saleman. Zita liked Johnnie because Joe-Joe liked him, and because almost every time he "came on" to Boston, he would throw a big lobster and beer bash at Margaret's house. Minnie, however, was another story. Because she came from Boston Street, right on the Dorchester line, the poor gal had three strikes against her the first time Joe-Joe met her. Didn't help that she "put on airs," and tried to one-up everyone. Zita? She flat didn't like Minnie, and that was that. But, being a good scout, Zita always tried keep up her game face.

Underwear was the usual sleepwear in our house prior to the Visit. However, Zita ruled that during the Visit, there would be a change. Everyone was to wear pajamas to bed. Going out to buy pajamas for three kids was obviously not in the budget. The domestic arts, including sewing, were not her strong suit. She had never met a sewing machine. However, to her credit, she was determined to put up a good front for Aunt Minnie, even if that meant that she had to make – read, sew by hand -- pajamas for the whole family.

One of my sisters must have been with her when she got the fabric. And, she must have had enough advance time to sew them the previous winter. Maybe that's why she bought flannel. But, white, with a printed pattern of pink bows? My first pair of pajamas like they wear in the movies, I complained, and I've got to wear pink bows?

Actually, it was kind of fun having another boy in the house. We slept together. Jackie didn't have any comic books, and he didn't like going out to play. But, he was learning to play cards, and it was fun having someone to talk with. Minnie would go out all day to visit with her sisters and shop in Downtown Boston.

Ma, do they have fudge cakes in Chicago? I asked mid-way into the Visit.

Why, I don't know. I would guess they do. Why do you ask?

"Well, Cousin Jackie told me that he's not sure if he likes fudge cake anymore. So, I was just thinking that Aunt Minnie and Uncle Johnnie must really miss fudge cake because every day when she comes back here from town, she brings a fudge cake."

It was true. Not occasionally, but every day that sweltering August she would bring a Dorothy Muriel's fudge cake, and with great fanfare – as if she had just whipped up from scratch a twelve-layer Bavarian torte -- put it on top of the refrigerator, to join the others in their cardboard boxes with the little cellophane window.

August that summer was especially hot. That's when I first recall hearing the term, dog days. Boxes of gooey, sticky, chocolatey gunk piled up in the summer heat. Now, Joe-Joe was notorious for his sweet tooth. His children had more than youthful enthusiasm for candies, ice cream, and dessert items. Uncle John and Cousin Jackie were also zestful about devouring anything with sugar. But, this was too much. Both families quit cold turkey, but the fudge cake kept multiplying.

Never once did we have fudge cake in the house after that summer.

The Michael J. Perkins School was the public elementary school in the midst of the project, fronting on Burke Street where we lived when we first came to the Old Colony, and backing up to East Ninth where we moved to get an extra bedroom after the Visit. It had a large play area that was also available to the housing project kids. Opening on the East Ninth Street side, it seemed to be surrounded by trees and greenery. The City Park Department ran summer programs for children there. The first summer on East Ninth Street seemed exciting because of the summer-camp like activities going on just across the street. It was so close that I could go, on my own, for those parts I liked, and stay home and read when they were doing things I didn't. Like sports.

The highlight of the summer was the costume contest.

Alright boys and girls, here are the first prizes for this year's Park Department Perkins School Costume Contest. The young playground worker held up the prize for the best girl's costume, This doll can be fed water out of a nursing bottle -- and then, then girls, she will need to have her diapers changed. Isn't that special? And, just look at her pinafore. So sweet. Some lucky girl is going to win this doll.

When she held up the next prize my heart leaped. For the best boy's costume, she said half-heartedly reading aloud the print on the box, we have this Flash Gordon ray gun.

She had me there. I had to have that gun.

It was dark-gray metal with a futuristic barrel sporting a triple collar at the end, and an adult-sized grip. The trigger could go into automatic mode and fire off a seemingly never-ending round of sparks, that were called rays. If a seven-year old boy could be capable of lust, I certainly lusted after that gun.

Either I had outgrown the many costumes that Aunts Anna and Margaret had given me for birthdays and Christmases, or, perhaps I had a different vision. I so desperately wanted to possess that ray gun, that I was determined to pull out all the stops to get it.

Flash Gordon and I could fend off the Germans with that, when they came to Castle Island, I dredged up a patriotic ploy.

What are you doing with my glass paperweight? Zita asked the day of the contest. That was a gift from Catherine Crehan. It's hand-blown glass. From Venice. Italy. You better not drop it!

Ma, I just need to borrow it, said her son, fixated on the prize. Do we have a plain white towel?

That afternoon, just before the appointed time for the contest to begin, a swami left Zita's apartment and walked across the street to the playground.

Improvising, in the heat of the July afternoon I had put my Indian print flannel bathrobe on backwards, wrapped a towel around my head, and gingerly – very gingerly -- carried my mother's glass globe paperweight.

When my father came home from work that afternoon, he was greeted with, Dad, look what I won! The counsellor said my costume was the most creative. I put the towel back. I took out the pins, so it's OK when you take a shower.

How I loved that gun! Years later, in the aftermath of 1968's horrific turmoil when I had two very young sons and felt I had to ban play guns from the house, I thought about that Flash Gordon ray gun, and briefly felt sorry for my boys.

Families in the project got to know each other. The women would have weekly card parties that rotated from house to house. My sisters and I could tell when it was Zita's turn because the house would get cleaned, and she would buy candy, peanuts, tonic, and make a cake. Yes, my mother who hated to cook would actually bake a cake. From a box, to be sure, but the woman would put it together and a real cake came out of the oven. All these goodies were strictly off limits to everyone in the family – especially the children.

The ladies would arrive punctually at seven. Several hands of cards played, gossip traded, while ginger ale and orange tonic were quaffed and table goodies were munched. Until a certain hour, usually around 9:30, when they would ceremoniously put the cards away and have coffee and cake -- and heightened gossip. They would usually all be gone by 10:30 or 10:45. Anything left over -- nuts, candy, cake, tonic – was for those of us kids who got up out of bed to help clean up after the card playing ladies.

Ladies' weekly card-club meeting in Zita's kitchen, 1954.

A word about Zita. I have alluded to her skills as a seamstress and as a hostess. But, there is more. Her namesake, the saint venerated as the "Little Cook," patroness of kitchens, was revered for hundreds of years in Italy as a champion of domestic workers. Our beloved Zita, however, must have had a different inspiration.

After a seven-year hiatus, Zita returned to her job as a claims adjuster for American Mutual the year that I began high school. Eleanor was charged with care of baby sister Kathleen, particularly over the lunch hour, when all Sister School pupils came home for lunch so that the good sisters could return to the convent for their main meal of the day.

No Betty Crocker, nevertheless, Zita was a persistent manager of her children's nutrition. Every Sunday afternoon without fail, she would assemble sixteen bologna and cheese sandwiches, wrap them, and consign them to the freezer for withdrawal during the week. One each for herself, the two girls, and me for Monday through Thursday. Thursday night she would make four tuna salad sandwiches for the same distribution. Tuna couldn't be frozen, she said.

Joe-Joe preferred to catch his lunch on the fly.

This feat of culinary organization was consistent with her style. One of the memorable things about this period, as rocky as things sometime were with Joe-Joe and his Problem, one of the ways Zita provided continuity and stability was through menu planning. No calendar was needed to know what day of the week it was when sitting down to supper. Every day of the week had its dedicated entrée.

No substitutions, please.

Zita's 46th birthday cake. Joe-Joe, Eleanor, Tommy O'Malley and Kathleen, 1954, Old Colony.

Sunday was always either roast beef or pot roast, served right after the last mass of the day, around 12:30. It was accompanied by mashed potatoes, carrots, and peas (like all green vegetables, canned). Monday was Sunday's leftovers. Tuesday was chicken fricassee (also canned) on toast with peas. Wednesday was Prince spaghetti day, *always* with meatballs (Chef Boyardee from the can). Thursday was meatloaf, mashed potatoes and peas. Friday was fish – haddock, cod, or mackerel – breaded with Shake 'n Bake and baked until as dry as possible – mashed potatoes and peas. When feeling adventurous, Zita would have me mix equal parts mayonnaise and sweet pickle relish to make tartar sauce. Saturday was frankfurters and (B&M) beans, and (canned) brown bread.

Reflecting her basically healthy menu preferences and her endless dieting were the desserts. She made Jello-O. She opened cans of fruit cocktail, or once in awhile cans of cling peaches or Bartlett pears. Sometimes the leftover peaches, pears, or fruit cocktail would be recycled as a point of interest in the Jell-O. Occasionally she made coffee Jell-O with leftover coffee. Today when we hear about Jell-O shots, they are usually laced with booze. Zita's coffee Jell-o was espresso on steroids.

Apparently, Joe-Joe loved Zita for reasons other than her culinary skills. He was known to surreptitiously partake of a late afternoon mocha frappe to blunt his appetite. Another coping mechanism was to bring home pastry for dessert – usually cakes, Boston crème pie, or cupcakes. But, after the Visit, never fudge cake. Such treats would be served in addition to, not in lieu of, the homemade Jell-O or hand-opened canned fruit. Of course, all meals were washed down with as much whole milk as could be ingested.

Holiday meals were just as rigidly proscribed. Thanksgiving, of course, was observed with turkey, mashed potatoes, carrots, and all the canned vegetables that could be opened – cranberry sauce included. Christmas was roast beef, Easter ham with canned pineapple doughnuts fastened to the sides with whole cloves, and July Fourth was salmon and canned peas.

Some weekends Zita would be inspired to put together Aunt Jemima pancakes, fresh from the box. Of course, wheat germ was added, and canned corn and anything else from the refrigerator that was not moving. But, when they stuck to the pan, then we had the drama, the noise. She would punish herself and the whole family with gusty verbal tirades. I don't think I heard such language again until I was in the navy. Once she got going at the skillet, however, Zita was hard to stop. Before she knew it she was piling up more than her own family could handle. Often we would have to go out to dragoon our friends walking by in the hallway or out in the back yard to come in and eat some pancakes. These fruits of the frying pan were smothered in Log Cabin "maple" syrup, which Zita would copy by having me stand over a pan of boiling water and sugar while I poured in a tablespoon of maple extract for flavoring. After everyone – including the mailman -- was served, she would have me pour the left over elixir in the Log Cabin bottle that was fast becoming a family heirloom.

Zita's other weekend idiosyncrasy was her solo Saturday morning breakfasts. Especially after having returned to work, when the girls and I were older and less likely to be waiting for her to make pancakes, she would start her day off by reheating yesterday's coffee and frying up hot Italian sausages and coarsely cut peppers with which to make a breakfast sandwich. People on the third floor of the next building knew when she was preparing this dish.

My mother was also interested in various health supplements. Her favorite, and consequently, the most ubiquitous was wheat germ. Besides pancakes, wheat germ found its way into meatloaf, scrambled eggs, bread crumbs – anything that was porous and not moving. Brewer's yeast was hot for a while. She also insisted on not wasting the nutrients in things like the water used to boil spinach: she drank it as a beverage. She also instructed us that milk was a food, not merely a beverage, and as such it should be chewed.

By now, gentle reader, you get the drift that Zita was not an early prototype of Martha Stewart, let alone a follower of Saint Zita of Lucca. Housework, cooking, sewing, the domestic arts in general made the woman yawn. The seven years of her stay-at-home mom routine were marked by voracious reading, copious worrying, but lots of love lavished on her husband and children. For Zita, the need of the money she could earn was a great cover for her to get back to what she really wanted to do. Put on her hat, get out the door and go to work, where she could spend the day with other adults. There was a decided sense of relief that day in September 1951, when Zita was finally able to leave the running of the household to her children, go out the door to the bus stop, get to work and spend her days resolving insurance claims.

The only distressed family in our building were the Finnegans, who lived directly above us. Five children from diapers to fourteen. He worked at Fore River Shipyard, she worked in the newsstand at South Station. The word from the local Greek chorus – the women who sat out on the steps -- was that Madame Finnegan did not *have* to work. Paul brought home a very good paycheck, they said, but *that one* liked getting all dolled up every day and meeting the sailors at South Station. It was hard for me to figure out what was so intriguing about meeting sailors that would bring Billies's mother out to work every day, when no other mother in the building worked – this was before Zita escaped to American Mutual.

All the Finnegan kids went to public schools. Because both parents worked, the kids were home alone a lot, and there tended be a lot of noise. The older girls, Theresa and Maureen, did their best to keep the younger boys Billie, Bobby, and Tim, in line, but they could still be heard -- something unusual.

The parents' bedroom was the one directly above mine. One night when Mr. Finnegan came home with perhaps a drop's worth more stumbling than usual, and Mrs. Finnegan was already in bed, there was quite a commotion. The upshot was someone falling or being pushed out of bed, and Mrs. Finnegan leaving after a lot of noise. She didn't just leave the room. She left. Shortly a cab stopped at the building, and with great drama, she left.

And never came back. Theresa, the oldest at fourteen, took over the role of mother, and she did fairly well for a while. She kept the kids more or less in line, there was food in the house, and laundry got done. Mr. Finnegan went to work every morning and came home every night.

Fast forward about four years. By this time, Maureen, about fourteen months younger than Theresa, had an after-school job in a restaurant over the bridge in Boston, and was dating a college boy who she met waiting tables. He seemed like a nice guy when she brought him around to play ball with her brothers.

Then, one day there was no Theresa. Disappeared. Vanished.

Not that it's any of my business, Zita, Mrs. Eastman said one day, but, I think what happened is simply that Theresa is fed up with kids and housework. Can't blame her, she's only seventeen. I heard that she went to live with her mother. Maybe she wanted to have enough time for a boy friend, too. Like Maureen."

The mother role shifted to understudy Maureen. Only a junior in high school, she had to take over. This meant that she also had to quit her job. She was determined to graduate. At that time Tim, the baby, was not yet in school, Bobby had just started, Billie hadn't made his First Holy Communion. Maureen was caught. She obviously wanted out, wanted to have her own life with College Boy, but she also had loyalties to her siblings, if not to her father.

Kathleen and girlfriends pile on Joe-Joe's 1948 Pontiac. More automobiles in 1954.

It took a while. Two to three years of struggling to keep the family together. But, Maureen did it. Maureen eventually married College Boy when he graduated. The newlyweds moved to an apartment in Dorchester and took the three young boys with them. Their father went to a rooming house in City Point.

College Boy went to law school, while Maureen worked part-time while she took care of her four men. Tim and Bobby, the younger two, completed the twelfth grade and went into the service -- the draft still being in effect. However, Billie didn't quite make it.

Soon after leaving the project, Billie ran away from his new home. After several months, and with the help of College Boy's brother who was a Boston cop, they found the missing teenager. Maureen was horrified at his appearance and behavior, but with a great deal of effort they forced him to come back to the apartment in Dorchester. The fix lasted only a fortnight. Then, he was gone again. Beyond his mid twenties, no one had any contact with him.

The Washington Village Branch Library was located at the edge of the project, a few blocks away from where we lived. It was in the basement. I first went with my mother, who was a regular customer. It was clean and neat in there, the floors were always waxed and shiny. There was an absence of smell. The adult section was on one side, young adults, teens, and children on the other. Zita helped me get a library card of my own. I was turned on to a variety of books, particularly historical fiction, that held my imagination and took me far from the confines of the project perimeters.

One was a historical novel called The Rebel and the Turncoat, by Malcolm Decker. Set in New York, during the British occupation in the years of the American Revolution, this story features Nathan Hale, Benedict Arnold, two beautiful girls, and a hero who appears as an apprentice bookseller.

For me, a farther trip was a series of books set in then current time, about a family and their dogs. Springer spaniels. They lived in a spacious house in the country and had an upstairs living room. There were descriptions of the house, of the meals the family shared together, and of the role that the dogs played in the life of the family.

While both reading experiences took me to places and times I had never been, perhaps it was the novel set a century and three quarters prior that was less of a suspension of disbelief.

Zita wasn't much of a shopper. She would do it as a chore, never as recreation – or even as exploration. More often she would make a list of essentials and send me to the Elm Farm, a mini super market on Dorchester Street, three blocks away. One frigid Saturday when Joe-Joe was out working, however, Zita asked Mrs. O'Toole across the hall to be aware of the girls, and she took me on the streetcar to Broadway to shop for food.

It was a miserable winter day. Carrying heavy bags of groceries through the bone-chilling cold, the slush congealing underfoot, while the dim winter sky spat a mixture of snow and sleet, I was done in after the first store. We must really need whatever it is that the stores here on Broadway have and the ones down on Dorchester Street don't, I complained. Otherwise Zita would never have gone out in that weather. Let alone drag her first-born, and only son with her.

The snow got much heavier, having squeezed out the sleet. I thought it would never be over-- the trudging through the snow and slush. The numbness in my fingers. Besides being cold and dreary, it was also difficult to get around. Dirty snow banks took away half the sidewalk space and narrowed the street crossing options. A passing truck doused mother and son in icy slush. I dreaded each step and was anxious to get back to my cozy, overheated room and whatever book I had taken out of the library.

Woody Allen's deepest philosophical observation was that 75% of life was just showing up. Zita's was that human nature is too much preoccupied with the downside of life, which obstructs our appreciation of life's wonders. She probably learned this first hand. After working almost twenty years to help support her parents and siblings, she married – relatively late – a man she loved, but who had no idea of how to earn a living. Starting a family in the crest of the Great Depression meant that she kept on working, while he floundered to find work here and there.

Zita was a gal who made the best of what life gave her. Resting her shopping bag on a snowbank that dismal afternoon she said, Look, Son, you know, sometimes, things are not as bad as they may seem. Sometimes we get all worked up about how bad we think things are, or are going to be, and most of the time, it's really not as bad as we think. Now, I've got a cure for the cold. Let's stop for a hot chocolate.

That didn't have to be repeated. From the slush on the sidewalk on Broadway, we found our way indoors to the warmth of Woolworth's lunch counter, and sat down. Heaven! There were pictures of hot turkey sandwiches, hamburgers, frankfurters, various ice cream concoctions. But it was the hot chocolate that sang out to us. It came with whipped cream on top and saltines on the side. I had had hot cocoa at home before. When Joe-Joe was in the mood he would take out the Baker's chocolate box and get to work at the stove. But, I had never before had hot chocolate out. And, never since has a cup of chocolate-flavored drink tasted so sublime. For whatever reason, ever since that Alaskan Saturday on gritty Broadway in South Boston, whenever life seems undoable, I remember having hot chocolate at Woolworth's with Zita, and the world always seems better.

Nothing is ever as bad as it could be.

Zita was right. It's not as bad as it could be. Especially when we work to make it so.

She didn't like to walk, but Zita would walk when she wanted to. Many weekday school evenings after supper, she would suggest going to Dorgan's for fried clams. After supper. Come to think of it, there were always four places at the table for this family of five. Zita would invariably eat on the fly. No wonder she was thinking of fried clams later on.

Since her husband could do without fried clams, and furthermore would rather go out for ice cream later, she would take her growing son with her. Except in really cold weather, when we would take the bus, we walked the six or so blocks to G Street. Made her feel better about treating herself. Dorgan's Captain's Room fronted on Columbia Road overlooking the ocean. Midway down G Street from East Eighth was a doorway for takeout. You rang the bell, they buzzed you into a tiled waiting room with windows looking on to the restaurant kitchen. Zita would order a small fried clam and a small French fry. We would walk home eating. Zita the clams, me the French fries.

Radio was the primary form of popular entertainment during World War II and the years immediately following. It was also a spark for a child's thriving interior life. There were the weekday afternoon soap operas "Backstage Wife," "Stella Dallas," and "One Man's Family." Comedy weeklies included "Baby Snooks" with Fanny Brice, "Our Miss Brooks" with Eve Arden, "Duffy's Tavern," "Meet Corliss Archer," "The Jack Benny Show," "Amos 'n Andy," "The Red Skelton Show," "The Fred Allen Show," among others. "The Lux Radio Theater" brought audio versions of popular movies, sometimes with the original stars. "The Shadow," "Sam Spade," "The Inner Sanctum," were among the thrillers.

Most of these were thirty-minute productions that came into millions of homes, usually live, including their advertising sponsors. Golden era radio presented its audience with the excitement of storytelling, but also the opportunity and the challenge to the listener to partner with the medium in creating the missing mental images.

As I got older, I had my own favorites. “The Lone Ranger” was on three times weekly. I could not miss any. It was sponsored by Cheerios. There were many special offers. Like the secret decoder ring that cost thirty-five cents and three cereal box tops. There was also the weather predictor ring that used real litmus paper. How I haunted the mailboxes in the front hallway until the package came from Battle Creek, Michigan!

I was also a fan of “Sky King,” “Straight Arrow,” “Jack Armstrong,” and other “boy” shows. My sisters liked the Saturday morning serials, especially the “Cinnamon Bear,” which I dismissed as unbearably sappy.

Once in a while, Zita and Joe-Joe would take the bus to Chinatown to eat at Ruby Fu’s. This was a special occasion for parents and children. Because the kids never went with them, the parents would always bring back packets of little gelatin nuggets covered with sesame seeds. Strange taste, but I liked them. My sisters didn’t.

One New Year’s Eve when they went to Chinatown, I was just getting over a case of chicken pox. I was not quite myself yet, but apparently in good enough shape to be left in charge of my two sisters. I turned the radio on after the girls were in bed, and was listening to a variation of Orson Wells’ “War of the Worlds.” Not aware of hearing the original, this one had Pompeii erupting in the present time. It was so convincing, and I was so distraught that I ran out into the hallway, knocked on doors to tell the neighbors that Pompeii had erupted and killed thousands of people, and urged them to watch out, because the calamity was coming our way.

You’re sopped through with sweat, Mrs. O’Toole said when she opened her door. You must still be sick. When she heard the report of the radio show, she said, Look, Joey, I’m a

Sicilian, my father came from a place not too far from that volcano, and I gotta tell you that it erupted a long, long time ago. A long time ago! And it hasn't lately. Not for many, many years. Now look, there's a lot else to worry about, but, do me a favor, will you? Forget about Pompeii." She then went in to check on the girls, and said that I should go to bed and she'd keep an ear on the door for my parents to get back. Disappointed with Mrs. O'Toole's disinterest, I waited on the edge of my bed for them to come home. The instant they came in the door, I assaulted them with the whole story. Joe-Joe wanted to know where was Pompeii. Zita put a wet towel on my forehead and put me to bed.

Lying there in the dark I wondered what happened to the sesame treats.

A new gastronomic treat came to South Boston after the War. Through the Italian grapevine, Zita's father heard that a pizza parlor was going to open in South Boston.

Pizza, what was that? his grandson wondered. Well, Grandpa said, pizza is an Italian treat. Most people didn't have their own ovens in my parents' time, he explained. They would do their bread-dough making at home, and then take it to a bakery or some other place with a shared oven to bake. So, when they had some dough left over, they would flatten it out and put some tomato sauce and cheese on top, bake it with the bread, and then eat it for lunch on the way home from the baking spot. Sometimes they would send it out into the fields for the husband to tide him over before supper.

Now that this Italian culinary delight was coming to my neighborhood, Zita, Grandpa, and I were among the first customers. Grandpa came all the way from Roxbury on the streetcar to introduce his daughter, now in her late thirties, to the marvels of this Neapolitan snack. We went to a storefront, off the beaten track, close to St. Augustine's School.

Sense of taste and smell are stronger in childhood, and we now know that the sense of smell is closely entangled with memory. Clearly, I had never smelled anything like that. And, what is more, as an adult every time I make or eat pizza, I still look for that mythic combination of mozzarella, oregano, and tomato that pervaded that afternoon in a storefront in South Boston. It must have been very much made to order, because I remember watching the cook-server-interpreter taking the order, walking over to the Coca-Cola ice chest, opening the top, and fishing a ball of dough out from the ice and "tonic," and then proceeding to roll it out.

Unlike many city kids today, I seemed to have had a sense of the city over the Broadway bridge. As a ten-year-old, I was traveling alone for a nickel each way to Roxbury to help Grandma Pelose with errands and household chores. I knew about Fenway Park, the Esplanade, the then new John Hancock building with weather signals on its steeple, and, of course City Hall. The old one on School Street that looked like a German Reichstag building. Museums were free in those days. I knew of two: the art museum and the Gardner.

When Aunt Madeline came in her car to take Zita and Joe-Joe and the children to the Gardner Museum, a whole new world opened up for me.

"This place has so many pieces of churches in it, but it wasn't a church," I reported to my friends the next day. "It has so many paintings hanging up like a museum, but it was somebody's home. This lady lived there. In the middle of winter you go there and see flowers in bloom, just like summertime. That's even better than when my Uncle John goes to Florida, because you didn't have to travel all that way; summer came to you, right in your own house. Mrs. Gardner must have been a very rich and a very lucky lady."

While there was certainly great interest – especially in the summer time, and especially on the part of boys – I don't recall working-class families being as consumed with sports as they seem today. We did a number of cultural things as a family. Summer evening Boston Pops concerts on the Esplanade were free, and accessible by public transportation. Joe-Joe seemed to like them better than Zita; we kids couldn't care less, but it was an activity.

During the nineteenth century, two local destinations were built at the termini of streetcar lines to encourage ridership: Franklin Park Zoo at the end of Columbia Road in Dorchester, and Norumbega Park at the end of Commonwealth Avenue in Newton. Both were also part of growing up in the city for generations of kids in the twentieth.

Much of the architecture at Franklin Park was intended to be evocative of other lands. The elephant house had an Asian flair, the lion's digs was supposed to make the visitor think of Africa, and the aviary building, or bird house, could have been a set for Turandot. Its Chinese motifs were hard to miss. During one trip to Franklin Park after Grandpa Pelose died, when she went to the bird house with Joe-Joe and the children, Zita became overwhelmed with emotion and had to leave the stuffy confines of the cage-filled atrium.

I can just see him here with me. We came here – he took me here -- so many times," she sobbed when Joe-Joe took her outside. He loved the peacocks. Pa was such a sweet man. O, how I miss him, Joe.

Of the four children in her own family, Zita seems to have been the closest to her father. She was also close – and dutiful -- to her mother. After Grandpa Pelose died, Delia moved in first with John on Mount Pleasant Avenue and later with Madeline in the Florence Nightingale, both within four trolley stops of each other on Dudley Street in Roxbury. In that Zita was the eldest, and a daughter, it would have been natural for her to take Delia. But, living in the project did not permit such an arrangement. So, Delia was stuck with her daughter-in-law from Tennessee.

After her five-day work week at American Mutual, Zita would spend her Saturday mornings visiting Delia, changing the dressings on her mother's feet, cutting her nails, and performing other daughterly duties – such as bringing an occasional bottle of port wine. This continued for twenty years even when Madeline moved to West Roxbury, until Delia was admitted to Milton View Nursing Home in Dorchester's Lower Mills. Zita still went every week, but someone else did the nurse's aide work. I hope she still brought the port. At the risk of jumping ahead in our story, it was at Milton View where Delia mer her first great-grandchild when I brought my infant son to visit.

Another of the highlights of the early project days was the year of the bike. Much to my sister Eleanor's chagrin – she wanted a pony, but that's another story. For my tenth birthday I got a bright, shining, brand new red Elgin bike, complete with a wire basket on the handlebars and a flashlight on the front fender. For weeks, every night after supper, Joe-Joe would take me out to the Strandway to practice riding. He would hold the seat, and walk, sometimes run beside me.

New trolley on Broadway, mid 1940s

We didn't have much of a track record of interactional activities, Joe-Joe and his only son. Didn't play catch. He did take me to the rodeo and to the circus, and to an occasional movie Downtown. That was fun. But we didn't play together. He probably didn't know how. After all, he was a boxer, not a ball player. Moreover, fathers in that period did not play with their sons the way their sons played with theirs. After all, what role model did Joe-Joe have? His father was right off the boat and worked all day on the railroad. Who knows what effect his mother's mental illness had on his parenting capacity.

Joe-Joe did take me to Fenway Park and to Braves Field, presumably to watch baseball. Even although he expected me to play ball like the other kids, he seemed not enthusiastic about the game itself, but disappointed that I was not a player.

But, he tried. Every night after supper, holding that bike seat until I got it. As aggravated as I would get with my father later on, I always knew my father was essentially on my side. I knew because of the way the man held that bike, telling me wordlessly that it was a father's job to bring his son to the point where he could pedal on his own. After all, isn't that how a father's role is different from a mother's?

Nevertheless, it must have been disappointing for him. His only son not interested in the midget boxing programs, not interested in sports in general. With prodding, I did join the parish softball team. Father Barry was the coach. He was patient and kind, but I couldn't hit a thing and was too heavy to run well. Father Barry was also the priest in charge of altar boys, so I didn't have much choice in sticking out the season.

Still wasn't much fun.

A few years later, Joe-Joe had somehow gotten a 1936 Buick that looked like it could have belonged to Al Capone. This was a big deal. The War was over, but cars were a rarity in South Boston, and even more so among project families. This was battleship gray with spare tires mounted alongside the chassis, and a hump shaped trunk. Upholstery was of the velvet pile variety, and the after-market radio that toggled on and off had remarkable sound quality.

One Saturday afternoon the family went for a drive to Houghton's Pond in Canton, at the foot of the Blue Hills. My best friend at the time was classmate Kevin Connolly whose parents were separated and lived with his mother and older brother over on Burke Street. He came with us. At one point, we were all some distance from the car, when Joe-Joe remembered that he had forgotten something, and asked Kevin and me to go back to the car to get it.

The road leading to the parking lot, all green leaves and trees, was dusty with its hard-packed dirt floor. I felt like a big shot opening the car door with the slim key, getting the forgotten object, and locking it again. Coming back, running, I was way behind Kevin. Joe-Joe, watching Kevin, turned to Zita with an expression of awe and said Look how light on his feet that kid is.

It was as if he had never seen a boy run like that before. While it was probably not intended, I took it as a reproach, and pretty much gave up trying to be an athlete on any level.

Truth is that I didn't need much of an excuse.

Joe-Joe did try to encourage me to go the gym at the Municipal Building on Broadway to learn how to play ball. There were basketball and handball courts there, and it was a magnet for local boys. He cajoled, nagged, teased, tried everything to get me to go. Finally, I agreed to give it a try. But, I pointed out, I don't have a pair of sneakers. A ten dollar bill in my pocket, I went out to Thom McAn's up on Broadway and bought a new pair of Keds, took the bus the few stops up Pill Hill to the Municipal Building.

Then something happened.

I couldn't get off that bus. I watched the Municipal Building go by and rode all the way to the end of the line, City Point. I just couldn't bring myself to get off. I could not bring myself to walk into that building alone, deal with the kids who were already there with their friends, and confront a new situation. Just opening my mouth would precipitate torrents of abuse because of my stutter. And I just couldn't risk being teased and rejected about my weight. What if some of the bigger kids from school were there, the ones always pushing me around, calling me "fairy," "fatso," and "queer?" I asked myself.

It was safer to stay on the bus.

I stayed on the bus until it came back to East Eighth Street, got off at my stop, went home with the new sneakers.

I told my father I couldn't find the Municipal Building. Joe-Joe was not amused.

Still from *The Phantom Empire,* a Mascot Serial, 1935.

Chapter Eight

The side of the mountain opened like an oversized garage door while a thundering horde of men clad in capes and space helmets rode their horses inside the earth en masse. Once there they traveled downward in cylindrical elevators 25,000 thousand miles toward the earth's core, to the location of the city of Murana.

Ruled by Queen Tika, the Muranians were a lost civilization tracing their history over 100,000 years to the to the sinking of the continent of Mu to the floor of the ocean, when their ancestors saved themselves by seeking refuge in caves. The Muranians were a highly advanced society, using robots for all physical work, leaving the citizens free to pursue the life of the mind in peace and tranquility.

Early twentieth-century views of futuristic technology are highlighted by wrist radios and two-way television systems for routine communication, and the predictor of the internet in the children's-wading-pool sized screen used to observe any aspect of the world above their subterranean kingdom. There are also the obligatory neon bolts of lightning and other holdovers from a Frankenstein film.

Picture Queen Tika, costumed not unlike the Infant of Prague, with rhinestone tiara, full cape and floor-length dress topped by a frilly neckpiece, sitting in her art deco throne room, and surrounded by a court of Muranians dressed in cast-offs from both biblical and science-fiction epics, many of her closest aides in headgear similar to bishop's miters, and perhaps you get a sense of the wackiness of this tale.

But wait, there's more. The location of Murana is in the Western United States, within an easy canter of Gene Autry's Radio Ranch. Autry's (business) partner has two children, who become his sidekicks. They start a club, whose members ride around on horseback with capes on their backs and tin pails on their heads. They also assist Gene in getting out of cliff-hanging scrapes and back to Radio Ranch by two p.m. every afternoon to broadcast his radio show, enabling him to keep both his contract and his ranch. Plus, we are treated to both seeing and hearing Gene's performance.

It may be that this serial was responsible for my cosmogony in those early years. Or was it the other way around? In my mind the globe was a physical representation of the outside of a sphere, within which, like the people of Murania, we all lived. The continents, oceans, skies -- everything – were all inside. Affixed to the underside of the globe's shell. Therefore, when everyone was complaining about Adolph Hitler and what a menace he was to the world, I couldn't understand why someone didn't just open the hatch of the globe – I was sure there was one somewhere -- and throw the Fuhrer out the hatch.

Twelve episodes of this science fiction meets singing cowboy serial were made by Mascot Films and released in 1935. A decade later it was still being shown to wildly appreciative audiences of children.

Every Saturday morning at 10:00 a.m., in the basement of the Old Colony Village Administration Building, a children's movie show was held. A group of boys from our building would go early to set up the folding metal chairs in rows facing the pull-down screen. We also stayed to take them down, but that was so much harder because we just couldn't wait to get outside and re-enact the story of the Phantom Empire.

Over the next couple of years, we graduated to the magnificence of the Broadway Theater. Daily matinees. Saturday specials for kids started before noon and didn't end until after four, with different stories to re-enact on the way home every week. Those were the days when you got two features, usually B westerns, a serial, cartoons, newsreels and of course, previews of coming attractions for 11 cents. To peg that against current values, 11 cents also bought a loaf of bread or a package of cigarettes.

During the War, the Broadway Theater was the site of Bond rallies. After the War, Tuesday night was dish night. Even although South Bostonians were not able to commit large amounts of money to buy War Bonds, the rallies were electric in their own way, and filled with vaudeville comedy and music acts. Dish night, by comparison, even discounting the patriotism that imbued this community, was flat, dull, and listless. Zita went to get out of the house. One time, she took me. Perhaps to get an extra piece of crockery. With every ticket bought, a plate, saucer, or cup was given. Depression glass, Jadeite, and whiteware where popular handouts. When the campaign began to get stale, they would also give bowls and perhaps a gravy boat. Ironically, some of this is today sold for much more per piece than today's admission cost of a first-run film.

Empty marquee of Broadway Theatre after closing, probably 1960s.

Another Mommy movie experience was when Zita and I went to a matinee showing of Spellbound. I was about 8 or 9. It was a Holy Day, no school for St. Augustine's. My two sisters weren't in school yet, so they stayed home with my father who was working nights at the time. Apparently, I wasn't quite used to adult fare. Things were boring, but not a problem through all the talk between Joseph Cotten and Ingrid Bergman, and the popcorn was a real treat in the middle of what should have been a school afternoon. Then, all of a sudden the tenement-sized screen became a monstrous vortex. It was rotating. The now famous Dali dream sequence of "Spellbound" startled me so much that my entire box of popcorn erupted over the two of us. A dime lost to cinematic history.

There were other shows in town. My little gang of kids was far more loyal to the pictures themselves than to the picture house. Especially as we got older -- fourth or fifth grade -- we would go to whichever movie house had the better show, usually a toss-up between the Broadway and the Strand, a nickel trolley-car ride away in City Point. In good weather we walked and spent the money on candy at the refreshment stand.

Wherever we went, we always came home re-enacting the movie, sometimes for days. Towels and pins weren't needed, much to Joe-Joe's appreciation.

By the sixth grade, things got more complicated because I had discovered Uphams Corner. I knew about Uphams Corner because Aunt Madeline lived very close by.

A two-trolley ride away, through Andrew Station, Uphams Corner had two movie houses across from one another on Columbia Road: the Strand (different from the Strand in South Boston) and the Uphams Corner. The latter had a very cosmopolitan policy of continuous shows starting at 11 am. Today's trend of moviemakers aiming at 14-year old boys because they tend to see the same picture more than once is mere codification of earlier reality. My friends and I spent many Saturdays watching two showings of epics like the "Black Rose" in one sitting. If that is not escapism, what is? Plus, we also paid only one admission.

As we progressed in cinematic sophistication and ventured outside the area to discover the two dozen downtown movie houses—including Washington Street's opulent movie palaces with first-run films, and the South Station cinema which showed only newsreels and short films in the railroad terminal–they were always compared to the experiences we had in that windowless chamber under the BHA Administration Building. Not the animated cartoons, Three Stooges and Abbott and Costello comedies, Dead-End Kids movies, not-so-new newsreels, or C-level oaters that could be seen elsewhere. But what I still remember is The Phantom Empire. None of the other weekly cliff-hangers I saw in the years following could compare with its hold on my imagination.

Perkin's Square looking down Dorchester Street, 1940s.

St. Augustine's May Procession, 1949.

Chapter Nine

There was a definite, very particular, Sister School smell Probably emanating from the sisters themselves.

Was it the soap that they scrubbed themselves with? More likely it was the starch that kept their wimples and other whites as stiff as plastic.

Whatever it was, it clearly distinguished Sister School classrooms from Public School.

But that was not all.

There was also the crucifix and the statue of the Blessed Mother and the Little Black Sambo that collected pennies for the missions.

And there was crepe paper. Crepe paper was around holy pictures made into Valentines that the nuns seemed to be selling year 'round. It was behind the classroom crèche at Christmastime, it was made into roses around the statue of the Virgin during her special month, May. Crepe paper was everywhere. Without crepe paper the May Procession would be impossible. Crepe paper was Catholic.

But there was also something else about the parochial school classroom in the 1940s: it was homey. It was warm, it was predictable, it was personal, it was constant.

Somehow you knew that when you went into a parochial school, it was a public place, in the sense of being open for all who chose to send their children there, but it was not a Public School. And that was because it belonged to the nuns. And, of course, the sisters belonged to God. It was an extension of their home, the convent. You felt as though you were entering a part of the church run by women religious.

It was their domain. That's why it was Sisters' School before it was Parochial School.

Sister Superior, who was also the principal of the school, was at the top of the hierarchy in this universe. She was the pastor of this subset of the parish. All the nuns deferred to her, even the maintenance man did. Every pupil in the school lived in fear of being sent to her office. Parents respected her authority. On those rare occasions when they were summoned to school, they invariably met her in the late afternoon – at the end of the blue-collar working day – in one of the parlors of the convent itself.

One of the finest achievements of American Catholicism in the last century was that of the parochial school. Waves of poor, working poor, immigrant children and their children were schooled by cohorts of young women – largely from the same stock as their pupils -- who gave their lives for their God and his people. To say that nuns were a source of cheap labor is an oversimplification, but it may be one explanation of how a poor people's church could achieve so much.

Catholic schools, hospitals, and institutions in this period were also showcases of the managerial prowess of women at a time when they were not as significant players in like public institutions. Even smaller and mid-sized parochial schools required great administrative ability. To begin with, there was a sizeable physical plant to maintain. Then, there was a workforce, a faculty of women who not only taught in the same building, but also lived together. They lived in community, a community of sisterhood. There was a pastor to deal with, who was usually the source of operating revenue for the school. There were the pupils – sometimes half of them were boys, which posed a whole new equation for this kind of faculty. Parents were like the audience you can't see beyond the footlights, but are aware that they are there because if they weren't, you wouldn't be on stage in the first place.

As generous as pastors and parishioners were in making possible the parochial school miracle, it was the sisters who really made it happen. That despite the paucity of resources and educational strategy, these women achieved such positive outcomes in the vast majority of children is the true miracle.

Authority helped. These were not mere women like your mother or your aunts, these were sisters. Not nuns. Nuns were cloistered, devoted to a life of prayer with no contact with the world. These were *sisters*, women religious who sought to make the world better by their work. Here, they were in charge. Like shamans in tribal cultures, they interpreted access to God. The priests, of course, were the direct link to God and to heaven, but the sisters were the on-the-ground traffic controllers who managed daily life for kids at mid-century. Their authority came from God and His church, we thought, and of course, their uniforms made their role instantly recognizable. They must be special people – not people, really, but *sisters* – or they wouldn't look like that.

You never saw a sister eating or taking a sip of water. Did they really have legs under all those yard goods? Cops and priests at least looked like men dressed in uniforms. Even the vestments on a priest seemed temporary because you've seen him on the street in just a suit, not even a cassock. Sometimes on the ball field in just a shirt. But the sisters? More like mermaids. Sort of half person and half something else.

There was dependence on rote memory over reasoning, and most parish schools got by with less than current materials and with insufficient equipment. A local parochial high school had one biology class microscope for 34 girls. What student ever, ever *wrote* in a book – even a workbook – in Sisters School? This worked not only because of the time and the place, but also because the teachers had unquestioned authority. As poorly educated as they were, the nuns had more schooling than the parents of their charges, and, they had something else: God. They were only behind the priests as the instruments of the Lord's word on the local scene, what it means, and how to be sure that we're on the right path to salvation.

No one questioned Sister. No one.

Sister Anthony taught third grade boys at St. Augustine's. She was a tall, kind and serious woman with slightly sallow skin, who moved with quiet grace. Penmanship was very important to Sister Anthony, who had been challenged with the level of Palmer Method skills that I brought to her when I came to her class at the start of the year. That he is left-handed is bad enough, Sister, she explained to her Sister Superior, We are changing that. But, those Sisters of Charity at

St. Joseph's over in Roxbury just did not prepare this child. He does not form his letters properly. His penmanship is not up to St. Augustine's standards.

What do you think we should do, Sister? asked the principal. June starts next week, the school year is gone.

Sister Superior, this is a boy who is young for the grade and very young for his age. He stutters. Sometimes badly. I think he would benefit from repeating the year. I could work on his handwriting, and perhaps confidence with the class materials might ease his speech impediment.

The next day, closing her books on the last class of the day, Sister Anthony called me up to her desk. This is a very important note for your parents, she said as she handed me a sealed white envelope. I felt the Dutch Linen stationery held between my thumb and index finger as if it were something right out of the oven. Both your father and your mother are to come to see me in the convent this afternoon at 5:30.

I looked at her in wonderment, looked at the mysterious envelope, responding automatically, Yes, Sister. I put the message in my green schoolbag and went home.

I stayed home with my two sisters when my parents went to see Sister in the convent's front parlor.

In a four-room project apartment there is not much that parents say that children cannot hear. When they returned from their meeting with Sister Anthony, Zita and Joe-Joe went over the gist of what Sister said in those twenty minutes in the convent.

How often parents of parochial school kids heard those words: *Sister said.* Sister said that the effort to change Joey from left-handed to right-handed was slower than she expected. No question, Sister said, that a child should be right-handed, regardless of how he started out. Sister said his penmanship is failing. Not proper Palmer Method. Too messy and hard to read. Sister said they are going to keep him back, have him repeat the third grade. Sister said it's not so bad. He was still young for his age and it would give him a chance to grow up a bit. He might even grow out of his stutter.

Since I was the only one of the kids in the family in school when we came to South Boston that previous summer, and since I had attended sisters' School in Roxbury, it seemed natural that I should go to St. Augustine's School. The sisters at St. Joseph's didn't seem to mind that I was left-handed. They taught me to write. They thought I was a bright boy.

What did they know?

They were Sisters of Charity.

St. Augustine's May Procession, 1949.

Fifty-five years prior, the pastor of St. Augustine's Church had invited the Sisters of Notre Dame de Namur to come and run a grade school in the parish. Later, a high school for girls only was added.

The school building was a big red brick hulk that dominated the corner of E and Eighth Streets. Boys and girls were in separate classrooms, with separate teachers, separate play yards. There was also the dress code. The girls wore skirts and blouses; the boys wore shirts and ties. Tradition had it that boys wore knickers until Confirmation; long pants after that. Practically, that meant that boys in grades one through six were usually in knickers and long stockings, and boys in seven and eight were in long pants -- which some found cooler in the winter.

Built in turn-of-the century mansion style, the convent was across the driveway from the coal chute through which the City of Boston routinely delivered free coal to a parochial school. The convent was fired from the same furnace. Realizing that parochial schools saved the City money, Mayor Curley saw to it that the same City truck delivered coal to all the schools in a neighborhood, public and parochial.

Joe-Joe grew up living as close to St. Augustine's School as his son did, and he started out there, but transferred to the Bigelow, the local public school, after a few years because he disliked being "pushed around" by the sisters. Zita was also a public school girl, as proud of her high school graduate status as she was of her friendships with so many different kinds of people in Roxbury.

No one, however, questioned Sister Anthony's belief that it was a good idea to force a left-handed child to write with his right hand. In her mind, the highest vocation her pupils could achieve was that of clerk. Handwriting was the cutting-edge skill in her view of the world. And, it was her job to make sure I was adequately equipped.

So, I had to listen to the same third grade lessons for a second year. Had to repeat the same Palmer Method drills for another straight year. Up, down. Push, pull. Circles, capital letters, small letters.

Because I was familiar with the material, Sister would often call on me to give answers to the class, to help distribute materials, and I was always one of the boys to clean the blackboards, stack books, and help Sister carry her bags to the convent. While there is no evidence that the extra year helped my penmanship, it didn't hurt, and it did help socially. After all, I had been enrolled in first grade – no pre-school – as soon as possible to relieve Delia – Grandma Pelose.

Moving on to the next grades, I probably did feel more comfortable, more in charge, and enjoyed being recognized as one of the smartest kids in the class. Stutter or no stutter.

There were times I could not go into a store because I feared I could not make myself understood without ridicule. The Elm Farm supermarket was fine, I could take the list Zita gave me and collect the items off the shelves. If I had to go to the First National and ask the clerk for something, or to the drugstore, I had a problem. Talking with kids who knew me well was usually fine, but those with whom I was less familiar was a real problem – sometimes brutally so.

In school, I actually liked the group drills – repeating the multiplication tables, answers to catechism questions – aloud and repetitively because my voice was lost in the class. Singing was fine. But offering spontaneous answers was a big problem.

Penmanship improved over time. Eventually, I became a right-handed child. By sixth grade my Monthly Palmer Specimens show a larger, firm, practiced, but ungraceful hand. Looks as though you're drawing, not writing. Loosen up! Joe-Joe told me. A book of spelling tests from the fall of the same year show many stars, high marks, but decided hesitation and lack of fluency. Not unlike my spoken communication.

Two years later, the October issue of the school newspaper, The Clarion, features a display of gratitude to the school's pastor for an infusion of improvements over the summer. Undoubtedly suggested by Sr. Ann Francesca, I wrote a letter thanking Fr. O'Connor for tarring the boys' schoolyard. The tar is soft and makes for an easy landing, I wrote. We don't have that lopsided cement to trip on. If a boy does trip, which would be a result of a foot put out purposely, or a loss of balance, he would suffer a shaken body and an excited heart, at the most.

The cranky Sister who took her midlife issues out on the kids is not wholly a fiction of stand-up comics and disaffected Catholics' war stories. While she had far fewer checks and balances on her authority than her public counterparts, she did have her counterparts in other systems.

Nevertheless, those stories are hard to forget, and they also tell us of the automatic respect the nuns enjoyed from parents. In the early 1950s, a girl who had just lost her mother transferred from a public junior high school to her close-by Catholic high school for girls. She was looking forward to the nurturing support of caring women living out their faith in service to their charges. First day of school in her new surroundings as she was basking in the warmth and special feelings of the smaller school run by another branch of the Sisters of Charity, she witnessed a jarring act of violence.

The class ahead of her was lined up, single file in the corridor. A girl was called out of line because she was thought to be harboring gum in her mouth. Apparently, the rule-breaking girl didn't give the right response to the inquiring sister, because the next thing the new girl sees is the nun pulling back her habit sleeve on her right arm, winding up, and punching the gum-chewer where the chaw had been, knocking out three front teeth.

Next day at school, the buzz was that the toothless girl's mother had been summoned to see Sister that afternoon. The mother reportedly thanked the haymaking sister for disciplining her daughter and told sister that the girl deserved it, and would get more punishment at home.

Fear is a primordial form of social control. Given large classes, isolated teachers, and minimal teacher education, it is a form that, by and large, worked effectively.

Corporal punishment was once a norm in public as well as parochial schools. The sisters were only doing what was always done, be it with the hand – open or closed – or with the ruler, the rattan, or even the clicker, that spindle looking thing held together with elastics that made the click signal when snapped. Because of their unique authority as teachers and as women religious, however, the sisters were able to get away with swatting kids longer than their counterparts in the public system.

Perhaps because their worlds were so small, a few of them often also indulged in vengeful and cruel behavior toward children.

It was a Thursday in November of 1947 and the circus was in town. I had signed up with the Boys' Club to go, along with several other kids from my fifth grade class. The teacher was Sister Iraneus. She was literally as wide as she was tall, had a mustache and a beard, and was among the most miserable people ever known to have set foot in a classroom. Sister was one of those nuns who gave women religious a terribly bad rep. She was known for punching boys severely because they looked at her the wrong way. In retrospect, she must have had a number of mental health issues to face as she said her morning hours.

The day of the circus trip, of which she was aware, was a Thursday. Thursday afternoons was Released Time in parochial schools -- time for the pagan kids from public school to come in and get religious instruction. For some infraction of Sister's Gestapo rules, the group going to the circus was punished by staying after school and writing I will always obey Sister 500 times in their best Palmer Method. Who knows? Maybe Sister wanted to go to the circus and was jealous. Whatever, we had to sit there and do it, not to leave until done. Sister sat at her desk guarding the door, correcting papers.

School was over on Thursdays at 1. I was due at the Boys' Club at ten of 2.

The fifth grade classroom was two flights of stairs and five blocks away from the Boys' Club. Tall windows along one wall, white globes of light suspended from lofty ceiling, green walls with an array of religious art fringed with crepe paper, an American flag, a statue of the Blessed Mother, Sister's desk on a raised platform at the front near the door, and two huge blackboards.

An introduction to stressful feelings of conflict regarding time erupted that afternoon. Sure, I wanted to go to the circus, what 10-year old boy didn't? But what was really bothering me was that the people at the Boys' Club were expecting me, they were counting on me to show up. After all, I had been saving money earned from collecting newspapers and empty bottles, baby-sitting Patty O'Toole next door, and hoarded allowance. There was no way for me to tell the Boys Club that I had a cockamamie teacher who wouldn't let me go. I was stuck. If I left before doing my 500-line penance, not only would I be in deep trouble at home, and would have an impossible time coming back, but I was convinced that this nun would probably also pummel me on the way out – if I could even get out, physically. If I stayed to complete the assignment, I was sure to miss the bus and let the Boys' Club down.

It was a miserably long afternoon.

Like Zita said, It's not always as bad as it seems. The evildoers plugged away, writing repetitive lines without meaning in composition books. It got to be 1:45, we were anxious, fidgety. Two o'clock came and we were despondent. Eventually, Sister told us to bring our composition books up to her one by one. She looked to see how much had been done. Then we sat down again. Time to clear the room for Released Time boys, Sister said abruptly as she stood up. You boys are to complete your assignment at home, and you will bring it in tomorrow. You will also tell your parents what you are doing and why. Perhaps then you may change your behavior. If not, mark my words, you will not complete this grade.

It really didn't matter to us that we had no idea why we were being punished. Feet didn't touch ground on the way to the Boys' Club, thinking for sure that it was too late, we had missed the trip. Arriving at the front stairs just as the other kids were coming out, we were just in time to get the bus and begin the trek in to North Station to see the circus at the Boston Garden.

I don't remember whether I ever completed my Palmer Method penance, or whether I told my parents – or what I did wrong, for that matter. What I do remember is the glorious make-believe world of the circus, and seeing it with my friends. Perhaps, in her perverse way, that was what Sister Iraneus was trying to do. Show us the value of shared experience. Just perhaps.

Pill Hill, Broadway, 1940s. Albanian Orthodox Cathedral, center.

There were also, on balance, many examples of tender consideration of which these hardworking and unappreciated women were capable. Another pupil's father, in my sixth grade teacher's absence, made a public mockery of me because of my weight. The adult had come in to talk to the class about planning a little surprise party for our teacher. Singling me out, he asked me to stand. Now see this boy? He's so fat he can give up ice cream for just a week and have enough money to pay for this surprise. Amid the class's raucous laughter and jibes, he told me to sit down and start saving.

As soon as Sister Bernadette heard about this, she pulled me aside and told me all the good things I had going. Look, you are a smart, hard-working boy. That man doesn't know you and doesn't know what he's talking about. There is no one in my class who can write better than you can, and who gets as high grades in history and religion. I know it's hard, it's embarrassing in front of the class, but forget about this. The outsides of our bodies tell nothing about what's inside. Your huskiness is something you may grow out of, but your insides – your mind, your soul, the way you care about others – will stay with you. You're going to be in good shape, son!

In the sixth grade, Sister Bernadette was such a relief after a year with Sr. Iraneus. Sister Bernadette was tall, somewhat tom-boyish, always flushed, positive, and very earnest. She was the Sister who astounded her class by telling them that their parents loved them. Many of us had never heard that before. Not from our parents. And not because they didn't love us. Probably because Dr. Spock's book wasn't out yet. She also told us that she had spoken to Ted Williams about his foul language, and he promised her that he would watch it. Sister Bernadette was very popular with her boys; on the order of a Big Sister.

A new boy in class. Something rare. The postwar exodus from the inner-city hadn't yet begun, and neither were families coming in to South Boston, so the kids you had in class, you had in class year after year, until you graduated. Like the small town it was. I was an exception when I came in third grade. Actually, a rare exception, because the war was still on. So, when Adi Georgian came, it was news. Plus, Adi was a D.P., a Displaced Person. He smelled of garlic at a time in which no one I knew used it. (Zita's Italian father having died by then.) Adi was orphaned in the war, and adopted by an ex-GI and his wife. They ran a boarding house on Broadway at the foot of Pill Hill.

Adi was a year or two older than most of the boys in class; he was still struggling in English. No English as a Second Language classes then, Adi learned by total immersion. Coming from Europe – Hungary, I think – Adi was also a great deal more sophisticated and worldly wise than the rest of us guys. Adi talked about sex. Suddenly, a classroom full of forty-four 13 and 14 year-olds seemed to be obsessed with sex. Not that we knew much about the subject. But, Adi did. And he had a lot to say.

By the time eighth grade came everyone was a lot more interested in the topic.

It is hard to know to what degree Sister's sex education program was prompted by Adi's disinformation strategy.

Here was a woman, probably at most in her early twenties, brought up in the late 1930s in a traditional, ultra lace-curtain, Irish family, who had committed herself to a celibate lifestyle through a Vocation, who was about to do something infinitely radical for her setting, her time, and her place.

Sister Ann Francesca was going to talk to eighth grade boys about sex. This is nineteen forty-nine.

The compounding dynamic was that there was not a boy in class who was not secretly in love with Sister. Middling height, slight build, and a beautiful face radiating from her wimple, Sister had very white skin -- except when she was flushed, which seemed to be a lot of the time – and very dark hair, if her eyebrows were a clue. I thought she looked like my favorite movie star at the time, Ann Blythe.

This was the sister who never had to carry her bags from the convent up the stairs to the third floor eighth-grade boys classroom. She never had to ask for help in cleaning the blackboards, mixing ink, clapping the erasers clean, sweeping the classroom, or any of the other teacher's classroom chores. We boys fought each other to be the ones to do them.

Now, remember, what happens this afternoon is only for here, Sister prefaced her symposium on sex. It is very, very, very important that your parents do not hear about this lesson.

Nor should your brothers or your sisters hear a word of this. You should not mention this to any other Sister in this school. Certainly, not one of the priests should know about this. After a pause, she added, As for the pastor, Monsignor O'Connor should never know about what happens this afternoon. Never.

Then, she pulled down the green shades on the tall classroom windows.

To this day, I cannot tell you what she told her class. What is remembered is her concern. Sister Ann Francesca was concerned that the boys' parents would not or could not address the subject of sex. As eighth graders preparing to leave the cloistered calm of Saint Augustine's Grammar School for a disparate range of high schools -- and some boys not going to school after that at all -- she didn't want her charges to hear the gutter version first.

As an aside, only three boys in that class actually continued in Catholic schools. One went to Boston College High, two to Cathedral. Most of those who went on with their education, went to South Boston High School, some to English High, or Boston Technical. No one went to Boston Latin. That was a public school track. Good school, yes, but, you know, it is not a Catholic school.

Sister's concern came through whatever her presentation was. All we remembered was something about the love between a father and a mother resulting in the birth of a baby. There were nudges and winks, and Adi tried to look as world-weary as possible, but we were all spellbound – Adi included. Whatever it was sister said.

I never forgot her. Neither did most of the boys in that room that special afternoon. Someone had cared enough about us to take a chance. The content, the whole issue of sex education, was far less important than the simple fact that someone in authority cared that much about us.

It was not only fear of bodily harm; it was also fear of eternal damnation that kept the pupils all in line. Religion class started the day. Baltimore Catechism reigned supreme. Who is God? Why did he make us? These were the baseline questions that were internalized.

Lives of the saints were also a big teaching tool. Somehow, a virulent anti-communism, personalized in anti-Stalinism, imbued many of the other subjects, notably history and geography. The sisters always prayed for the conversion of Russia, and urged the pupils to do likewise.

In addition to the warmth and personal atmosphere of parochial school that was important to so many hordes of kids in the project neighborhood, the other really important aspect was constancy. This included the invariable routine of the school day and week, its predictability. For youngsters whose home life was sometimes in turmoil, school becomes a touchstone to stability. Each pupil knew what to expect once we set foot in school. We also knew what was expected of us.

In addition to the school work itself, it also was expected that the children of St. Augustine's were patriotic. Monsignor O'Connor had acquired huge loudspeakers that were placed in open classroom windows so that the entire school could march out to Souza melodies blaring loud, every day, twice a day: going home for lunch, and at dismissal.

Each school day began the same way in each classroom: with a Pledge of Allegiance to the Flag, recitation of the Preamble to the Constitution, and then morning prayers.

Saint Augustine boys and girls were expected to make the school proud of them by being helpful to their parents at home, and kind to their brothers and sisters. It was mandatory to attend Sunday mass with the class. Attendance was taken. Boys not seen on Sunday had to bring a note from home before being re-admitted to school. Everyone was expected to attend daily mass at least during Advent, Lent, and the month of Our Mother, May. Weekday masses were celebrated in the lower church, in the basement, a few steps below grade – which was still a foot or two above street level, because the building was perched on a little knoll.

Despite the full-sized windows, the place was still not the cheeriest place on the block. Wall space not covered with stations of the cross, windows, or altars was painted a shade of yellow-cream disturbingly close to that used on every interior in the project. The three altars and the rail fencing them off from the congregation were a combination of wood painted a faux marble, and the stone itself, all in a grayish white. Entering from the doors closer to Dorchester Street, worshippers had to pass by a full-scale replica of the Pieta – again, grayish white -- surrounded by jumbo, economy-size vigil lights in blue and red holders. These cost more – ten times as much – as the smaller variety at the altar rail.

Very often there would be a Month's Mind, or other memorial, which meant that music would be disrupting the meditations and general wool-gathering in which the boys and girls engaged during these horrendously early rituals. Mass was in Latin, there were no homilies during the week, so there was no incentive to stay awake. When I was feeling guilty and trying to make sense of what was going on, I would often attempt to ascribe meaning to the sung Latin pieces. The soprano would change, but there was nothing I could make out of anything that person sang, whoever she was. The tenor, however, was always Mr. Stack, the sexton. He was a burly gentleman with gray wavy hair combed back like Joe-Joe's. I was convinced I understood one piece he sang before Communion at every mass.

Are You Stayyyy-ing? Kwee toll-is bekatah mundee, mumble mumble.

Are You Stayyyy-ing? Kwee toll-is bekatah mundee, mumble mumble

Are You Stayyyy-ing? Do-nah know-bees ba-shemm, mumble mumble

To get yourself ready for Communion, I thought that this piece was asking Our Lord to stay with the communicant after the sacrament was over. If only Mr. Stack wouldn't mumble after Are You Staying, maybe I could get more, I thought. I looked forward to it as one of parts of the mass I could understand. Each time I tried to figure out a little more.

Being an altar boy later on didn't help either, since there were no translations for the phonetic sounds we learned as Latin responses to the priests invocations. How was I to know that Mr. Stack was singing the Agnus Dei.

St. Augustine's Girl Scout Troop, 1954. Eleanor third row far left.

It was also expected that pupils and their parents would help the sisters in raising money to keep the school going. There was no tuition. The school had spaghetti suppers, minstrel shows, and other vehicles for social integration and fundraising. Some of the children enjoyed going to door to door selling chances. Little white booklets of raffle tickets had to be sold by students and parents. Parents bought what they could, but rarely had interest in selling. The sisters urged me to go up to City Point where the money was, to sell chances. How I would hate ringing doorbells and asking complete strangers to give me money. Was I going to stutter? Would they laugh at me?

The school also produced a newspaper, the Clarion, to which this reluctant salesman contributed articles, and a cover sketch of Pope Pius XII that I traced from the newspaper.

The constancy of parochial schools also included knowing that the same kid who sat beside you in third grade would usually be in your classroom the next year. And the next, until graduation. Whether you liked that kid or not, whether he was even a friend as opposed to just in your class, you knew him. Really knew him. Especially in a city neighborhood, that was an important method of assimilation and socialization. You didn't have to like or socialize with a kid who you knew, you could just know him.

Very few project households were particularly religious in a spiritual sense. As immigrants and children of immigrants during the Great Depression and World War II years, we were Catholic the way gang members were Sharks or Jets. It was who we were. Very few among the blue-collar, working poor, ethnics had had rigorous Catholic education, or knew much about the faith that we embraced. For the children, parochial schools were a vibrant introduction to the Church.

Memorizing catechism questions for school quizzes became parent evangelization when Sister suggested that pupils have at least one of their parents hear the rote responses. For most of them, it was new ground. The mass was in Latin. Even although most Catholics went to mass on Sunday, they most often said the rosary or at best meditated before and after the sermon that was almost always about the Blessed Mother. Very few had prayer books with seasonal daily and weekly readings in English, with which to follow along. Furthermore, it was not unusual for some groups of men to get dressed up for church, go to the church building and hang around outside catching up with their friends on the latest doings, and not go inside.

Mayor James Michael Curley (left), Richard Cardinal Cushing (right).

In a project parish, similar to medieval times, the Church was the center of the community. It was the hub of all education, the locus of worship, and the integrating social institution. It was also the core of most local political campaigns. The Holy Name Society, the Sodality, the Boy Scouts, the altar boys, the various novenas and missions, minstrel shows and spaghetti suppers, were all social vehicles to bind an increasingly diverse ethnic parish in a social whole. In addition to boys in my room with Irish names, there were many Poles, Lithuanians, Slovaks, Albanians, and Italians. For kids then, especially for us kids coming from the projects, the Church as seen through the parochial school was a magical thing.

The parish church was more than the repository of knowledge, the sanctuary, it was also the place that was the pinnacle of the visual and performing arts. Where project buildings were as blandly uniform as Sino-Soviet housing was in the decades following, every church building in town was different. Where parishioners homes were small spaces filled with right angles and hard edges, the Church was a vast interior space of curving timbers, rococo plaster, and luminous multi-colored narrative windows, in the midst of which was the chiaroscuro of flickering tapers and the particular scent of stale incense.

Also like the Middle Ages, with James Michael Curley as mayor and Cardinal Richard J. Cushing as archbishop, Catholic Christianity in the city had become a civic tapestry that was a backdrop for all events major and minor.

May processions were perhaps among the most public displays of Catholic religiosity. Not as extensive as the annual St. Patrick's Day Parade, but still covering several blocks in a circuitous route from the school to the church, the May procession attracted full sidewalks along the route.

Every kid in the school from first grade through the senior class of the girls-only high school was in the annual May procession -- which must have caused the felling of a forest just to make the crepe paper. The idea was to escort the statue of the Blessed Virgin to the church so she could be crowned (with crepe paper roses, what else?) after a prayer service including recitation of the rosary and benediction of the Most Blessed Sacrament.

My last year as a "civilian," the second go-round in third-grade class, was representing the doctors of the Church. We wore purple smock-like crepe-paper gowns with crepe-paper hats. The next year, I proudly walked with the altar boys

accompanying the Blessed Sacrament. Our cassocks and surplices were cloth.
The majesty of Catholic ritual, the richly embroidered and colorful vestments, the mystery of the Latin said and sung, the back-of-the nostrils scent of incense, and the familiar music seemed awe-inspiring. Before becoming an altar boy, I would often play church, just as I played the movies I had seen. My room had both a statue of the Virgin with its own miniature grotto and blue votive candleholder, and it had a somewhat larger statue of the Sacred Heart. That meant that I could begin in May with special services to the Blessed Mother in her month, and continue through June, the month school got out that was also dedicated to the Sacred Heart. Because my sisters were not only little, but they were also girls, I usually found one of my friends from school to assist me in these rites. Johnny Shaughnessy was the most frequent acolyte. He eventually became a priest.

Guess I did something right.

Older trolley coming into Andrew Square Station, 1946.

A Holy Thursday custom then was that of the pilgrimage of the seven churches. In the later years at St. Augustine's, my buddies from school and I would often undertake this pilgrimage on foot. Starting at St. Augustine's, we would walk to St. Brigid's, Gate of Heaven, St. Peter's Lithuanian, St. Monica's, St. Mary's Polish, and St. Vincent's. We were hardly alone. Several clusters of people along the age spectrum were doing the same thing, walking the streets of Southie on a cold April night. With the same enthusiasm with which we rated baseball players, we discussed the varying styles of decoration used by the different parishes on their respective altars of repose for the Blessed Sacrament. What can I say? Most of us were altar boys.

Boys, there is something you should know, announced fourth grade teacher Sister Agnes Patrice. One of the very special and grown-up things about fourth grade here at St. Augustine's is that this is the time for new altar boys to begin their training. Some of the kids looked at each other apprehensively Now, as you know, Father Barry, our newest curate, is in charge of the altar boys. He has asked me to send him our very best candidates, she said as she looked around the room. By next Thursday. What will I be looking for, you wonder? More eye contact around the room. Naturally, the boys I recommend will be doing well here in class, that's a given. It is after all, a very special honor to assist the priest at the holy sacrifice of the mass. Boys who are on the altar with the priest have got to be serious, well-behaved pupils. Clean hands – including fingernails – are a must. Most of us were not too surreptitiously checking out our hands and nails. Punctuality is extremely important. It would be foolish for me to send Father Barry a boy who has trouble getting to school on time, wouldn't it? Forty-four heads nodded. Once your name is on that mass schedule, you must be there. And, be there at least twenty minutes early! Why? To change into cassock and surplice, get the water and wine from the rectory and light the candles. Which means that, if you had the quarter of six mass, you must be there at what time, Mr. Richardson?

Wakened from his reverie, a pupil in the third row looked up, Uh, in the morning, Sister?

Of course, the morning, John. You'd have to be there at what time?"

Um, quarter after five, Sister.

Well, I suppose you could be there that early, John, but twenty minutes is sufficient. Twenty-five after five.

Having commanded their attention once again, she continued. Additionally, these boys would have to learn Latin, so that they can give the responses."

Sister, a hand shot up. Does that mean after-school lessons?

Father Barry will take care of the Latin. Now, the boys who succeed in passing his Latin test would begin training with the older, experienced boys under Father Barry's supervision, of course. Those boys would be required to purchase their own surplice. Remember that the surplice is to be kept clean, pressed, and freshly starched. Mothers do that for you. Cassocks are provided by the parish, handed on from boy to boy. Shoes will be polished, and, of course, your hair will be neatly combed.

There was buzz at recess about the prospect of being altar boys, and who would be chosen.

Thursday came, and to my surprise, I was among the half dozen or so chosen to meet with Father Barry in the sacristy of the lower church right after school.

Gerard Barry was a tall, lean, light-haired, earnest young man who had grown up in Newton Centre, and was just finding his way in the inner-city. After introducing himself and asking each of the boys to tell him their names, he distributed pasteboard cards produced by a nationally known church supply house. This is the hardest part of this job, he told his charges. The Latin. But, fortunately, we have a little short cut.

The front and back of the cards contained all the responses required of altar boys at mass. The priest's words in light faced type, and the boys' in bold. Everything was spelled phonetically, resembling the sounds of the Latin responses to the mass.

Ad day-um kwee lay-tiff-ee-katt yoo-ven-too-tem may-am. Was the response to

In-tro-ee-bo ad al-tar-ay day-ee.

Making Pig Latin seem sophisticated. There was no explanation of what the sounds meant.

When my father told his best friend, Joe Heirty that I had passed the test and would be an altar boy, Heirty, who had a son a bit older than me, and in public school and therefore not eligible for altar boy status, said, Well, it must have been easy for him learning the Latin, Zita being Italian and all.

There seemed to be a hierarchy in assigning boys to serve mass. There were three daily masses, plus from two to six funerals each week. The new kids, who usually had to train as supernumeraries with older boys, tended to have the earlier masses, and only got a wedding or funeral if requested by the family involved. Successful senior altar boys routinely were assigned the funeral and wedding masses. Funerals that happened during school hours meant that the altar boys were excused from class, to return to school right after the mass, feeling like big shots with their surplices over their arms.

Weddings were usually Saturdays, and never in Advent or Lent. Weddings and funerals were considered to be plums because they came with a cash gift. Funerals on school days were a double gift.

There were other perks. Some kids rode the subway into the Franciscan shrine on Arch Street to serve mass for a stipend of $2.00. Some, like Johnny Saunders and I walked up to Carney Hospital where we performed acolyte duties in the chapel. No cash, but the priest took us in town to the movies every once in awhile, and home in a taxi. Now, driver, they'll get out here, the priest would say when we were a few blocks away from our part of the project, I don't want the neighbors to think these guys are drunken sailors.

Not counted among the 2,212 performances of the hit musical, "Oklahoma!" is the 1946 version put on by St. Augustine's Grammar School. Could it be because the good sisters, just perhaps, did not get permission from the copyright holders? It could be that sisters didn't have to get permission? Also it could be because it was such a triumph that it put Broadway in shadows by comparison.

Thinking back, what were those sisters thinking about? "Poor Jud is Daid," the scene in which Curly, the hero, tries to incite his rival to kill himself to insure community approval (this is *not* made up!) must have registered with them as a no-no in Catholic teachings. It's a wonder that they even let us kids hum the tunes, let alone reprise the production in a revue. A revue that they revived for several years after that.

Including the year a few years later that the costume coach showed third-grade girls the kind of hat that they had to wear. Naturally, in sister school, everyone was responsible for their own costumes. The headgear in question was a cowboy hat with pom-poms around the rim. My younger sister saw bells rather than pom-poms. Are you sure about the bells, Eleanor, her mother asked, hoping that the answer was no.

Nevertheless, Zita hand-sewed the rim of her daughter's sombrero with three dozen little silver bells. The Jingle Bell kind that now adorn Christmas stockings. Her daughter was thrilled. Proudly, little Eleanor wore the hat to school the day of the dress rehearsal, shaking her head to the tune of "The Farmer and the Cowman" as she walked to school, causing quite a stir on West Eighth Street. How sad she was when the Sister Producer had to tell her that bells were not what she wanted in her "Oklahoma!"

How sad was Zita when she had to go up to Broadway to buy a yard of stupid pom-poms, strip off the bells, and sew on the pom-poms. Quite sad.

Anyway, here we are, the war is just about over, the GIs are coming home, and everyone is focused on how to get back to where we were before the Japanese blew up Pearl Harbor, and *the* big hit of the nation is a musical about the Oklahoma territory in 1906 and the love triangle of a cowboy, a farm hand, and pretty girl. Like we skipped two score years.

So, the capstone of my fourth grade was the school play in early June, a version of the most popular show in the USA, "Oklahoma!" Every child in the school was involved, ensuring that every parent would buy a ticket and come to see the show in one of its four performances in the auditorium at the sweltering top of the school. Technically – and perhaps this is how the sisters got off – it was not a production of the musical. It was a revue, featuring the hit tunes that happened to be from "Oklahoma!" "O What a Beautiful Morning," "I Cain't Say No," "People Will Say We're in Love," "The Farmer and the Cowman," Oklahoma!," and "The Surrey with the Fringe on

Top" were among the airs on people's lips that year, and among the numbers in the show.

Each of the eight grades in the school was given a song to present. The fourth grade boys and girls – all eighty-six of us combined -- were featured in the popular hit, "The Surrey with the Fringe on Top." Against a backdrop of blue skies and crepe paper clouds, a posse of cowboys – the boys – trooped on stage from the left, making a V with an army of farmer's daughters – the girls from across the hall – as a buggy with a crepe-paper fringe was hauled on stage by four eighth grade boys, including one who would go on to write a sports column for the Boston Globe.

To the refrains of "The Surrey with the Fringe on Top," one boy at a time from the cowboys line would meet one girl at a time from the farmer's line at the front of the stage, join hands, take off their hats, bow to the audience and then exit to their respective sides.

Ah, sweet kismet! The girl who I was paired with was none other than Michaela Shannon, my neighbor. I was beside myself with joy. I was embarrassed. I scrubbed my fingernails. I bathed the rest of me. I didn't want the other kids to know. I made sure my costume was as cowboy as possible.

Sunday night, at the end of the run, Mishy still hadn't reacted to my taking her hand on stage. She never did. Perhaps that fueled my fascination with her.

Chapter Ten

The author and friends at St. Augustine's Grammar School Graduation, 1951.

The bride's family has asked that you serve the eleven o'clock wedding two weeks from Saturday, Father Barry told me. Joe Heirty's daughter Patsy was marrying a police officer. Being a seventh grader made me a senior boy, meaning I could have my choice of roles at the mass. Bells or censor? Master of ceremonies? I asked myself.

These were the days of fasting before receiving Holy Communion. Not just a mere hour, but a complete fast starting at midnight. I had had no food since my routine peanut butter on Ritz crackers and milk snack before bed the night before. This was an eleven o'clock mass. It was an unusually hot day in early June, one in which the newspapers were talking about a U.S. "police action" in Korea. Not that I had the vaguest idea where Korea was.

I decided on the bells. In red velvet-trimmed cassock and starched surplice over usual street clothes, including shirt and tie, I knelt and sweltered on the marble step of the high altar, in full view of the entire congregation. I know I was supposed to be concentrating on the mass, and what the priest was doing. But, it was hard not to look out to see who was there. Not only the Heirtys and Joe-Joe and Zita, but all of the Heirtys friends who were by and large also friends of my parents. And, it seemed, every cop in Boston.

The bride and groom were kneeling on prei deis just outside the altar rail. Father Toland, the curate with the golden voice, was the celebrant. Mass was just about half over. The marriage vows had been exchanged. Sermon was over. Sounds of the organ had receded to a calm vibrato, the church was hushed as the priest was singing preface to the most sacred part of the mass, the consecration. Vere dignum et justum est, aequum. . .

Crack! I heard a tremendous thud!

Things went black, and the next thing I knew, two of the police officers from the congregation were standing over me in the sacristy. He's opening his eyes. Kid, you awright? one of them asked, undoing my tie as I lay prone on a bench.

Yeah, not only did you pass out, but you did some real damage to that step, the other one said . You came down with such a loud crack when you hit your head on the marble, you woke everyone up, kid.

I could hear that the ceremony had gone on without me. Father Toland had resumed the mass when I was hauled off the altar and into the sacristy. After a glass of water, I stood up, a bit dazed. Show must go on, right, kid? said one of the cops as he helped retie my tie and button my cassock. Then I came back out on the altar, positioning myself as quietly as possible at a kneeler behind the junior boy who had smugly taken over the bells position.

Nevertheless, after mass the Best Man handed the recovering acolyte an envelope with $2.

Zita and Joe-Joe were waiting when I left the church. They walked me home before they went on to the reception. We just want to be sure you're not going to keel over again, my father told me. Forget about it. There's lotsa times I wished I could just pass out when I was in the ring. Happens to everyone.

Now, son, are you really sure you're okay to stay with your sisters while we're at the reception? Zita inquired, not really expecting an answer.

It was Joe-Joe's idea that his son join the Boys' Club. On Sixth Street, it was about halfway between the project and Grandpa Doolin's. Today the specialty would be called after-school programs. Woodworking, basketball, cooking, music lessons, swimming, summer day camp, and trips during the school year to special events like the circus. They had movies too, on Thursday afternoons. But, after the cooking classes, what I really liked was the opportunity to learn to play a musical instrumcnt.

Zita had played the violin through high school, and Nana still had the instrument. I wanted to learn the piano, but staying after school to practice every day on the piano there sounded like a pain. No one had pianos in there houses, that I knew of. That was only in the movies.

The sisters had previously taught me to read music. Well, Gregorian chant, anyway. But it was fairly easy to pick it up. Just add another line and make the notes round instead of square.

You sound just like Jack Benny, my father told me.

You just need to practice more, Zita pointed out. At least three hours a day.

Zita, cut it out. What he needs to do is go out and play ball.

I didn't like swimming at the Boys' Club because they made you take all your clothes off. All. It was in the nude. Perhaps there was concern about the germs inherent in bathing suits. Germs or no germs, I sorely missed my bathing suit.

Not only was I conscious of being a fat kid, I was also awkward. First time I went to swim, I took off all my clothes in the locker room as instructed, and looked around for the entrance to the pool. Out in the hall, I had noticed a sign that said Pool Room. Still sopping wet from the shower, and quite undressed, I opened the door and entered the Pool Room, where the older and fully dressed billiard players got quite a hoot and chased me out with their cues.

One fall, baseball warm-up jackets were the rage. Even then, kids seem to have been defined by their jackets. As a fourth grader, I was very proud of my brand-new winter jacket of thermal nylon the color – and sheen -- of bronze. But four years later I was coveting a maroon felt jacket with Boston Braves written on it. Obviously, early logo craze.

Finally, one night I came in late from hanging out with my new friends all the way over in the Old Harbor project, and my parents were already in bed. It was a Friday night. The plan was to go in town with friends and buy the new jacket first thing Saturday morning, but I needed more money than I had. So, I peeked into my parents room to see if they were awake. Heavy snoring from Joe-Joe's side said he wasn't. Too late to ask him. My mother was a lighter sleeper – and an easier touch as well.

My buddies and I were Downtown that Saturday morning before the stores opened, our noses pressed to the window of Jordan Marsh department store that displayed the baseball jackets. As soon as the doors opened, we were first to scoop up our treasures and get back home so we could put our new jackets on.

Come winter, I really enjoyed the jacket. Until one day I came downstairs from serving a funeral mass in the upstairs church to find my prized new jacket gone from the row of coat hooks in the vestibule where the altar boys hung their things. How I liked that jacket! Now it was gone. I half ran, half walked the few blocks to school. Sister Ann Francesca asked one of the other boys in class to lend me their jacket so that I could go home, get another one, and come back.

But I didn't have another one, so I came back to school in my Easter overcoat that was a hand-me-down from cousin Franny.

Joe-Joe was adamant that the parish should replace the pilfered jacket. He insisted that I go to see Father O'Connor and request compensation. Sitting in the rectory waiting room to see the pastor, I squirmed in nervous anticipation. As often as I had been in and out of the church to serve mass, I had never been in the rectory -- except the connecting hallway where they kept the water and wine in an icebox. Just the idea of talking to the pastor was enough to tense up every nerve in my plump pre-teen body. Any kid who served a Father O'Connor mass knew how cranky he could be. Perhaps it was the power.

This was a period in which pastors reigned supreme. There were five priests assigned to St. Augustine's parish. Besides Monsignor O'Connor there were Fathers Toland, Cusack, Redding, and Barry. But it was the pastor who was the final authority. on everything from what we believed as Catholics, to who could sell newspapers outside church. He alone was responsible for taking in the money that came in the collection basket, and spending it. Being a Catholic pastor then meant that parish funds were your money. No parish council. Little diocesan oversight.

While it was little known at the time, Msgr. O'Connor, while pastor of a project parish in the Lower End of South Boston, acquired a summer home in Pocasset, Massachusetts. In an area popular with the families of successful Yankee businessmen, Msgr. O'Connor's summer getaway was situated directly on the water, and included a large house and outbuildings. On his death the property was left to the Archdiocese.

It was known that Msgr. O'Connor was a good friend of the new Archbishop of New York, Francis J. Spellman, making frequent trips to Manhattan to assist him.

There I sat in the rectory hallway, a nervous wreck, looking at the poster on the wall charting the various religious groups in the world, with of course, Catholics as the largest.

Finally, my turn came, and I went in to the office to see the pastor.

I c-c-came down from serving m-m-mass, Monsignor, and it was . . . wasn't there anymore, I explained.

What wasn't there?

My coat.

What kind of coat was this?

M-m-maroon j-jacket. With B-b-braves emblem on the f-f-front. B-b-brand new.

As business like the exchange was, I was never sure that the pastor really believed that I had had a jacket to lose. Or, maybe he remembered the laudatory letter in the school paper that October. Anyway, he wrote out a check for twelve dollars, and I was on my way.

My first real job was the summer I turned 14. Previously, I had worked as a babysitter and also made money by collecting and cashing in newspapers and empty bottles . During the War, America discovered recycling. Used paper goods -- newspapers, magazines – were in great demand for the war effort. Paper drives were held in which parishes and neighborhoods (most often the same geography) would collect newspapers and donate them for the cause. Since people were trained, after the war, young entrepreneurs like myself would go door to door collecting newspapers to be sold by the pound to a local paper recycling plant. Often, I would also collect empty milk and tonic bottles for the deposit.

But this was a real job. Mr. O'Toole, a next-door neighbor, was a U.S. Customs officer assigned to the terminals near Castle Island. I had baby-sat his two older boys. Being aware of some strain in his neighbor's household, O'Toole hired me virtually the instant I turned 14, the legal working age, to be a customs laborer. That meant that I would go to work with him in his car, then join a team of middle-aged men who were drilling bales of wool with hollow bores to collect samples. The bales were labeled Argentina, Venezuela, and Uruguay. This test would ascertain the presence of material other than wool that might be subject to import taxes.

Most of my co-workers lived in City Point. None had cars, and Mr. O'Toole would often give them a lift home after work. Most times, they were dropped off at the corner bar as a prelude to going home. I learned a lot that summer before high school. A lot about work and about workingmen's attitudes toward work and toward each other. I also learned that I didn't think I wanted to do that kind of work as a career. I was paid well, however, and liked the idea of working.

That fall, Zita went back to work. She rejoined American Mutual, and my sister Eleanor was in charge of helping our younger sister Kathleen at lunch time. I started high school and liked the idea of working so much that I looked for a part time job after school.

Zita and the Weber's cow, Condon's Bernice Claire Farm, 1947.

Chapter Eleven

Neighborhood politicians in the 1940s seemed to have paid attention to James Michael Curley's success in getting the support of the poor and the downtrodden. It didn't hurt that so many families – in some cases, whole districts – were in need of help as Boston and the nation stumbled out of the Great Depression. Whether it was giving mops to charladies so they wouldn't have to scrub floors on their knees, expanding public hospitals, or building public bathhouses, those seeking elective office realized that Curley's concern for the poor paid off at the ballot box.

A maintenance man at the South Boston Health Center on Dorchester Street near Broadway became a local hero by giving away soaps, detergents, and light bulbs. No one ever asked where these commodities came from, but in days of rationing, scarce jobs, and little money, people welcomed whatever largess flowed their way.

He was personable, presentable, and he could "talk." Eventually a State Representative's seat became open, and Jimmy Condon decided to run for it. He had a novel campaign gimmick for that day: fresh air. Condon had a pre-War wooden-clad beach wagon, but he also had a destination, he owned property in the town of North Easton, Massachusetts. Little more than twenty-five miles or three quarters of an hour on good roads from South Boston today, sixty years ago this was a meandering trip dangerously near that place where travelers fell off the turtle's back, taking longer than it now takes to get from Boston to Cape Cod on a typical summer day. Going to alternate parts of the district, Jimmy filled his wagon with project kids and took them to spend a summer's day at his "farm" in the bucolic town of North Easton.

In the years immediately after the War, North Easton and surrounding towns – Stoughton, Bridgewater, Norton, Raynham, Avon, Mansfield – had small family farms that were still operating. Most of the farmers, however, also worked at the local shoe factory or other light industry. The Bernice Claire Farm – named after Condon's daughter – was not a farm, however, but a house and a bit of land. But, it was out in the country, so by project standards it was a farm. Built in the late eighteenth century as an inn on Bay Road, the old carriage route to Brockton, the house was a square, wood-frame classic

Federalist statement close to the road. It did have a large open field and pine grove in the rear, but no livestock, no outbuildings.

However, the Webers next door did run a dairy farm. The smell of cows, hay, manure, fresh warm milk, pigs and their slop, were all in the air. For a city boy to be suddenly immersed in country smells, was a new and intense adventure. The woods between the Bernice Claire Farm house and the pine grove smelled miraculously of a pungent green, the essence of the color green, mingled with a mangy earthy scent of soil dampened and kept damp by tall, overhanging trees.

The pine grove was a place for adults to shoot rifles at empty bottles and cans and drink beer. I didn't get any beer, but I did learn how to operate a .22 caliber rifle, and was disappointed that it was not as much fun as my Flash Gordon ray gun. Kids played the same games they played in the city, but we seemed to get tired faster, in spite of the relative coolness. There was a pond for swimming in Norton, a few minutes away by beach wagon. For the boys, there was a swimming hole within walking distance. The food was sublime. Hot dogs, hamburgers, corn on the cob -- all cooked outdoors over an open fire.

The summer of 1946 I went to Condon's farm with my family many weekends. Jimmy Condon and Joe Heirty were friends. Heirty was my father's best friend. Heirty introduced Joe-Joe to Jimmy, and everyone seemed to be become fast friends. So much so, that as Jimmy contemplated the management of the farm for the next summer, 1947, he asked Joe-Joe and Zita to come and spend the summer there, as a family. Jimmy's wife Helen didn't like staying there for long periods, his secretary was too young, and he needed someone to be a continuous presence in the house for the stream of kids and the occasional parents who would come to spend the day.

There were tenants upstairs, the Cooks, but they worked all day and were not home, except for Freddy, who was a couple of years older than me and -- until the end of the summer when he ran out of kids his own age -- avoided me.

The day came to begin the summer hiatus in the country. Jimmy came to the house. The Heirtys were in the car, Joe, Theresa and young Jay were going for the day. The wagon was loaded with people and clothes. Zita had taken the girls to Pober's the week before to make sure they had pinafores, bathing suits, and enough underwear. There were five adults and four children in the vehicle. It was full. Most of my family's clothing for the long rural summer was packed in cardboard boxes and strapped on the roof of the wagon. Years later, on reading the scene in *Grapes of Wrath*, where the Joads set out for the West, I recalled that trip from South Boston to Easton.

Although narrow, the Ford wagon had a third bench, and Jimmy often bragged that he had gotten as many as 23 kids in it. Evidently those were skinny kids, not like those in the wagon on this voyage.

Stopping the safari at a mid-way point for gas. we realized that there was nothing on the roof. The new summer clothes that Uncle John bought for my sisters and my mother the previous year, were gone with the wind -- along with things new this year. My things, and my father's things were in shopping bags inside the wagon. Not an auspicious start to a new summer experience. Suddenly experts in driving, the adults complained about Jimmy Condon's "cowboy at the wheel" performance.

Once ensconced at the Farm, I completely forgot about the project, and couldn't even remember what my room there looked like. Especially after making friends with the Weber kids at the farm next door, I got into the rhythm of summer in the country. I helped them with their morning chores of feeding and watering and milking the cows. I learned how to collect eggs from the hen house without getting pecked. The pigs didn't need care, they seemed to live off the residue of the family table. We played games in the interior darkness of the huge hay-filled barn, jumping from rafters into the abyss of bales of stale grass, inhaling the special perfume of enclosed hay. As the summer grew old, we picked berries in the woods and gathered vegetables from Mrs. Weber's garden.

Weber's barn next door to Condon's Bernice Claire Farm, 1947.

I also helped Jimmy orient the kids who came on the wagon for day trips, I helped my mother prepare the cookouts, and also helped the adults set up their rifle practice targets in the pine grove.

Long and languid days of summer taught me so much about the outdoors. Crops of day lilies and Queen Anne's lace had replaced the playing fields and beach in my familiar urban landscape – although I knew the pond and the swimming hole could never replace the magic of the ocean. I learned how to catch fireflies in jars with holes in the cover so they wouldn't die. Country things. The closest store was a mile and three quarters up the road. There we found a small general store, gas pump out front, and two elderly gentlemen surveying the world from rockers on the porch. To any and every lost traveler, stopping for directions, the response in unison was invariably, Up the road a piece. Bottled Nehi grape tonic pulled frigid out of the ice chest that said Drink Moxie, and popsicles of any color were all the rage that summer. Country things.

Joe-Joe had just recently started his full-time, permanent, City job, but did not yet own an automobile. He who had not ever in his life gone more than a mile to get to work, traveled by public transportation from North Easton to Boston and back every day that summer, leaving the house in the dark of early morning, to return at twilight. For me and my sisters, it was a stretching exposure to a way of life very different from that which we knew in the city. Certainly much more of a respite than the kids who just came for the day. For my parents, separated from European existence farming by a single generation, it must have been just as revealing, and perhaps gave them even more appreciation of their own parents. For Jimmy Condon, he won the rep's seat and held it for years to come.

Zita and Joe-Joe at a wedding, c. 1948.

Chapter Twelve

They went to a wedding, my parents.

I baby-sat my two sisters.

They came home late for a morning wedding.

Around seven.

When they came in I knew there was something wrong. My father was stumbling, my mother was guiding him to the bedroom. I see my father near the closet curtains by their bed, fumbling with his clothes. She had to help him get undressed.

He even smelled funny.

This was the big, strong man who could do anything. A boxer, he could swim, drive a car, teach a boy to ride a bike.

I asked my mother what was wrong. She said nothing, just that he had had too much to drink.

One evening after supper that summer, Joe-Joe went to the package store and brought back a bottle of whiskey. He must have been celebrating something, because he made drinks for the people sitting out on the stairs.

Ordinarily, he never went out to sit with them. He would meet one of his friends and go for a walk. But, sit on the stairs? Never. He would usually brush by with a frown and a grunted greeting and go in the house. Tonight, he was out there -- host of the stairs --drinking with them.

My bedroom window faced the stairs. Whether I wanted to or not, I could hear everything that was said. Life in public housing meant that children hear everything that happens, everything that is said in their own apartments, and usually in those adjacent. We grew up fast. My father must have behaved particularly silly that evening, because I did something very rash to intervene.

I was probably just nine at the time.

Joe-Joe kept the liquor in the linen closet near the bathroom door. Zita also kept shampoo there. People didn't usually wash their hair every day then. I combined them. I poured some shampoo in the booze.

Next night, when my father was mixing post-prandial drinks, I decided it would be a nice night to get out of the house. When I returned about an hour later, my father was quite upset, talking about getting a bad bottle from the package store. I said nothing. Disgruntled and embarrassed in front of the neighbors, Joe-Joe took the bottle's remains up the street to talk to the store owner about the defective dosage.

He came back sputtering and more red-faced than when he left, saying that the man said that because Joe-Joe broke the seal himself, whatever tampering must have happened in his house.

That's when the nine-year-old confessed. I told my father that I added shampoo so that he wouldn't drink the whiskey and make a fool of himself again.

It was a long time after that that I noticed my father drinking again.

Joe-Joe got a part-time job at the German Club, a major social center in town, located just beyond the project on the way to City Point. He was friendly with the owner, who needed a relief bartender.

The new bartender's story was that because so many of his friends came in who wanted to buy him a drink – and of course, to say no would be an insult and bad for his friend the owner -- that he just had to oblige.

This is when the "benders" began.

He wouldn't come home. Zita didn't know where he was. It was too late at night to call the owner. Tears, prayers, worry. Back on the knees by the bed sobbing before the same crucifix. I was sent to look in the German Club and other places where my father was thought to be. Many times. The only time I ever found him, he was on a barstool just up the street. Maybe I was ten by then, but apparently not too shy to go in and tell Dad that Ma wanted him home.

It was worse in later years when he had a car.

Then I had to look for the car, too.

One time Joe-Joe was aware that he hit something with the car. Somehow, after the accident he got the car to the gas station on Broadway near the bank, and left it there. Smashed fender and all, Joe-Joe went on partying. A few days later when he came to, and went to look for the car, I told him I had found it and it looked bad. But, I was too young to know about the legal aspects of such an incident. My father depended upon a local politician to help him fix this kind of problem, and once again his friend and future neighbor, Joe Moakley, came through. And, eventually, the car itself was also repaired and parked outside the house again.

Joe-Joe with City Councilor and Mrs. Joe Moakley, 1960.

Days at a time he would be gone. Zita was not a calm person by nature. She was a born worrier. Her son became her confidant – whether I wanted to or not. She had no girl friends, and she and her sister Madeline didn't talk about things like that. They talked about food, their mother, and their sisters-in-law. In that order.

When he would surface, he was barely human, rheumy-eyed, disheveled, incoherent. Back. Once he was vertical again, he would bend over backwards to redeem himself in the eyes of his family. He would make a big deal of washing and drying dishes, picking up Zita at work so she wouldn't have to take the bus all twenty blocks home. Then, he would be super strict with the girls. But first of all, he would call his boss. He worked as a Paving Inspector for the City of Boston, so he couldn't get fired. When he called, he would always lie and say that he was sick. They knew. He knew that they knew. But everyone was happier that way.

The family didn't know if it was worse when he disappeared, and we had days and nights of anguish, or when he turned up. By that time he was literally sick. And he was miserable. In the small apartment it was impossible to escape the din of thrashing and moaning as he dried out cold turkey. The dry heaves, the bile, the cries for relief. The promises. The deals. Everyone heard it and lived it with him, whether they wanted to or not.

Mother and son had an unspoken pact. We would carry forth the fiction to the two sisters that he *was* physically sick. We both tried very hard to shield the girls from the fact that their father had a problem with alcohol.

As a boy, I treasured the memories of Christmas when I was very little. Not only the Christmas Eve rounds of visits and the gifts from the Aunts, but in those days my father didn't drink much. From the time I was about ten, however, I absolutely hated holidays. Christmas I hated most of all.

It seemed that Dad would look for excuses to drink. Holidays, eves of holidays, vacations, all were prime escape hatches. Because Zita would get so hysterical, I would get apprehensive and nervous with the approach of Thanksgiving and Christmas. The noise and the fuss, the upset, the insecurity were rattling for me as a child. How I dreaded the sight of a Christmas tree, hated to hear carols. I just tried to hold my breath until the holidays were over, and my father was more or less back to "normal."

And, they fought. Noisily and bitterly. Zita swore worse than he did. I worried about what would become of me and my sisters if our parents split up. Not that that happened much in our world, but wives did throw husbands out of the house, as I witnessed in the apartment above me. My family was always so pressed for money, I couldn't imagine how we would cope without my father's City paycheck.

Gradually, I began to assume a parental role with my sisters. By the time I was in high school, my after-school job bought back-to-school clothes for them, Christmas gifts, and Easter baskets. After all, they were little girls and I thought they were being cheated out of nice things and cheated out of being children.

All of this did not help enrich father-son relations. My unfortunate lack of interest in sports, my failure to live up to Joe-Joe's expectations of his only son as a regular Southie kid, were problematic enough, but it was the overlay of my father's excessive drinking that drove us apart. Words were very few between us. Our relationship had ceased to be that of a father and a son. For years it was more like two begrudging roomers in the same quarters, mediated by the woman of the house. Behind it all, I never hated my father, but I no longer respected him. I was terribly ashamed of him, embarrassed for him, and hurt that he could be so unthinking to my mother.

The girls were younger and didn't see the world the way a son did. They had better relations with Dad, and that was fine with their brother. At this point I just wanted out of that house and to get on with my own life.

It was symbiotic, however.

My family needed me to continue the fine balance of managing a drunk, and meeting expenses, and I needed someplace to live so I could continue going to school. As committed as I was to working, somehow I knew that I had to keep plugging away at school at the same time. Above all, I was determined to get out of the project, and on with my life.

Whatever that was.

Decades later, when I visited a refugee camp in Africa to prepare for the absorption of five dozen of the Lost Boys of Kakuma, through Catholic Charities, I thought of those days. In the culture of these boys' home, the Sudan, one is either a student or a worker. One either spends all day washing dishes or digging ditches, or one spends all day studying. Never both. The boys recoiled when told that in America, they would be expected to do both at the same time.

These young men had been through years of travail and turmoil. They left their homeland in the face of a 30-year war. They marched away and were strafed by their own government. They sought refuge in Uganda, which turned them away. They walked thousands of miles as they witnessed most of their number perish in floods, famine, animal attacks; the girls raped and stolen for concubinage, the boys captured and transformed into gun-toting members of the Sudanese Liberation Army as young as ten years old.

But they balked at working and studying at the same time!

When told that many Americans do just that, they reacted as if they had been told that many Americans fly to the moon every weekend.

A boy at midcentury, I was caught in a symbiotic relationship -- as most family relationships are.

Somehow, I didn't resent my situation. It was what it was. No one asked whether Joe-Joe's behavior was connected to his mother's mental illness. It was what it was.

I felt fortunate to live in a time and place that made possible the pursuit of my academic goals while I worked. Boston had a number of commuter schools that were relatively affordable at that time. Sadly, today it is much more difficult.

As for my father, Joe-Joe became more controlled in his binges as he aged. Luckily for both of us, we reconciled after I married. I was able to forgive my father, and tell him I loved him with a public kiss on the cheek, before he died suddenly at age 60.

Joe-Joe was disappointed that his son was not an athlete, wouldn't carry on his name in the Golden Glove and other amateur sports circuits. He felt he even lost out on having a son to go to boxing matches with, like his cronies. But, there was a vignette in the hallway in the project as my family was getting ready to move out and up to City Point that shed another light on his feelings. This was about a week after one of my old playmates from the building had been arraigned for stealing tires from a garage in Charlestown.

The accused thief's father was coming downstairs as Joe-Joe was taking out a box of crockery to the car. So, Joe, it's not just that you people are moving up to lace-curtain country, but look at how well you've done otherwise!

What do you mean, Dan? asked Joe-Joe.

Just look at it. Your kids have never been in trouble, have they? And then, to top it all off, your boy is going to Boston University while mine is in jail. They both grew up in the same place, here. What the hell did I do wrong?

Joe-Joe was proud to have a son graduating from college, going on to Naval Officers' Candidates School, who was, as he told a friend, as smart as a whip.

Perhaps that made up for not being quick on my feet.

It was complicated. I did love my father.

I did hate what he had become and what he did to our family.

However, we survived.

In retrospect, Joe-Joe was correct in calling it an illness. And I do not regret being complicit in that diagnosis.

Cathedral of the Holy Cross, High school is to left of picture.

Chapter Thirteen

I am sure I will get in. No question about it. Next year this time, I'll be at B. C. High and on my way, while you two guys are still floundering around.

Jimmy Dunn's two older sisters – who had raised him since his mother died when he was a toddler -- were determined that he go to Boston College High School.

Founded by the Jesuits in the Civil War years to educate the sons of immigrants, B. C. High was known for its rigorous classical college preparatory program. That's what Jimmy's sisters wanted for their future physician.

Remember, boys, for those of you going on to Catholic high schools, I have to have the name of your school by June 1, Sr. Anne Francesca reminded her class, or else we cannot guarantee that the school will get our certificate in time to hold your seat for September. I know it is a big decision. Talk with your parents. As I have said, I am available to review what I know about the schools with you. You can also talk with one of the priests. The important thing is to get the best education you can.

At this point in my life – an eighth-grader facing the choice of a high school -- there was no one charting a course for me. My parents in many ways behaved more like immigrants than children of immigrants. They provided for the physical needs of their children, cared very much about our futures, but did not presume to exert influence on our behavior, or on life choices. Their attitude was that the child should discover the new world on his or her own, and make the best of it.

Having no more than a sixth-grade education himself, and having floundered for more than ten years into married life to find steady, full-time employment, Joe-Joe was much more interested in job security for his son, than academic achievement.

Furthermore, the increasing and bitter estrangement between us devalued any opinions he would have offered his son. Zita's world view was the clerical workplace. She had had relative success and security in her career with a major insurance company, had enjoyed the camaraderie of her fellow workers. Because completion of a high school degree was essential for this kind of a job, she expected that her children would graduate.

She thought that it was utterly remarkable that, after many years taking courses part-time, her brother John had graduated from Boston University with a degree in business administration. Made him a big deal in the army, but she didn't see how it would help him once the war was over.

The teachers at St. Augustine's school were primarily concerned that their departing eighth grade boys go on to high school, preferably a Catholic one. Because Latin School was a public school, it was not on the sisters' list. South Boston High School, just up the hill from where I lived, was on their list – as something to be avoided at all costs.

Of the choices among Catholic high schools admitting boys, it came down to geography. If there was any bias at all, it was anti-B.C.High, primarily because it was run by Jesuits – who were priests. There was that tacit priest-nun competition.

Cathedral High School was taught by a different group of women religious -- the Sisters of Saint Joseph – from those at St. Augustine's, which had Sisters of Notre Dame de Namur. Each community wore different habits and had slightly different emphases. This was a full generation before sisters got out of their heavy black habits accented by white wimples and bibs that had so much starch they could have been plastic. My friend Ronnie from the Old Harbor project was going to Cathedral. They offered a general program heavily slanted toward business, as well as a college preparatory track.

Both B. C. and Cathedral High were located in the South End (B. C. High had not yet completed its move to Dorchester), accessible by a trolley and bus trip from South Boston. Although it was the location of the home church of the Archdiocese of Boston, the South End was Boston's skid row.

At midcentury, hundreds of handsome South End pre-Civil War brick row houses had been converted to tiny apartments, rooming houses, and flophouses. The elevated railway dominated the main thoroughfare, Washington Street, darkening sidewalks and storefronts at midday, and interrupting services at the Cathedral. There were sleazy bars, pawn shops, pool halls, and greasy spoons. It was a magnet for alcoholics, those on the way down, and those who preyed on them.

Gentrification may have been a few decades away, but there were still evidences of neighborhood life in the South End. Irish, Italians, and Germans were ceding turf to Syrians, Lebanese, and Turks, as they moved on to Dorchester and Quincy, usually skipping Roxbury entirely. The Red Fez and Harpoot's restaurants were local and metropolitan draws for Turkish and Lebanese food. French, German, Italian, and Greek Orthodox parishes still had enough congregants to pay the bills. Shops along the main drags of Washington Street and Tremont Street were ample and busy.

For those of you from outside Cathedral parish, bellowed my home-room teacher on the first day of high school, I want to say a few things about our neighborhood. Now, this is something that the students who attended Cathedral Elementary School, and have lived in the area know. Something that their parents tell them, I am sure. This area right around the Cathedral is fine. Boston police pay extra attention to this area. But, when you go a few blocks towards Northampton, she gestured towards the left side of the school, "or towards Dover Street, towards the right, it is important to watch your step. Watch your step, that's all I say. And, always, always take the bus. It leaves you off right at the corner of Union Park Street. Doesn't cost any more. When you come to school in the morning, and going home in the afternoon, if for any reason you have to walk to or from the Elevated, walk directly. And do not even *think* of looking in the doorways of the barrooms. Also, it is a good idea to find someone to walk with. If you absolutely have to walk, that is.

And, boys, as for the pool halls . . . need I tell you that any Cathedral boy caught in one of those places is automatically expelled.

Otherwise, there was no great concern about thirteen and fourteen-year-old kids going to school in that area. Stay away from the bars and pool halls. Move quickly. That was it. Parents did not lose any sleep over the safety of their little darlings in Boston's skid row. Part of Boston mid-century life for children included moving about the city relatively freely and without adult guidance. For me, it was no big deal. I had been going to my grandmother's house in Roxbury alone since I was nine.

The student body at Cathedral High School was markedly different from that at St. Augustine's. Of the roughly 70 incoming freshmen in 1951, fewer than two dozen had gone to Cathedral Elementary School. Of those, about half came from families who were long-time South Enders. There were a few Puerto Rican kids. By this time African-Americans had long begun their move from their historic Boston base in the South End to Roxbury and Dorchester, as Jewish families moved out of those areas. While there were a few blacks among the upperclassmen, there were none in the freshman class. Most freshman students came from Dorchester, Charlestown, West Roxbury, and three or four from South Boston. One guy came from Needham, which was regarded then as a remote outpost. A few came from Quincy and Milton – little better.

As big a difference as the mix in people, was the gender mix: girls were in the same classroom with boys. The coeds wore green sack-shaped uniforms expressly designed to disguise the human form. Guys wore shirts, ties, jackets

The latter was the only addition to the St. Augustine's costume for boys. Some boys left their jackets in their locker and came and went in more fashionable street styles, like bomber jackets.

Being an urban high school built in the 1920s, Cathedral High had no auditorium and no gymnasium. Smaller assemblies were held in the cafeteria in the school basement, larger ones across the street at the 2700-seat Cathedral of the Holy Cross. Basketball was played at the nearby Boston Arena.

Not quite a "Happy Days" set, LaLoose's Spa served as the local gathering spot. It was across Washington Street from the Cathedral and run by a Near Eastern family. The two boys from St. Augustine's – Ronnie and I -- didn't discover it until our first winter at high school, when it became the logical place to get a cup of coffee and a doughnut after the compulsory 7:00 a.m. Lenten daily mass in the basement chapel of the Cathedral. The crockery at LaLooses was older and heavier than Gerry's, a coffee shop near the Old Harbor, the coffee was darker and more assertive. The Art Deco mirror and stainless steel interior was a set made for Hopper. The place was larger and deeper than Joe's Spa or Gerry's, with swarthy countermen who wore pressed white linen jackets and ties.

The music on the juke box was a revelation. The Lucky Strike Hit Parade tunes and standards comprised the fare at Gerrys. Here I was introduced to jazz and rhythm and blues, which dominated the selections. Charlie Barnett, Cootie Williams, Count Basie, Sarah Vaughn, Slim Gaillard, and Fats Domino were among the new sounds. I found out about

Symphony Sid, who broadcast nightly from the Hi Hat nightclub, just around the corner on Massachusetts Avenue. Symphony Sid Torin's show combined unflagging advocacy for jazz and rhythm and blues with an intimate patter about the Boston music scene.

There were a number of small jazz clubs around the South End that drew a largely black clientele The larger ones like the Savoy and the Hi Hat, while staffed by blacks, had a mixed following. Several blocks away, the even larger clubs playing Big Band and Swing, tended to have performers and patrons who were almost exclusively white.

That's it. I am definitely not going back to school. I got a good job this summer, and I'm not giving it up, Ronnie sputtered. What good does a high school diploma do anyway? I can make as much now, and not have to put up with those bitchy sisters.

It was ironic that after choosing Cathedral because another guy from St. Augustine's was going there, by the start of the sophomore year I was making the trip alone. It turned out that Ronnie's primary interest in school was getting dressed up and being seen. At fourteen he was old enough to drop out and get a job. Ronnie was much more typical of Southie kids at that time than was the friend he left behind, for whom there was no option to graduating.

However, in the middle of the sophomore year, I, too, had had it with Cathedral High and the sisters. By that time, the novelty of high school – and coeducation -- had worn off and I began to realize that I might have been better off at the Jesuit High School. The decision I made a year and a half before, however, was based not on academic challenge, nor even on what school my friend from St. Augustine's had chosen. It was based on the ease of getting by. Not taking the risk of being in over my head, and avoiding, at all costs, the exposure of a speech impediment. Convinced that with the Jesuits I would be forced to participate in small group learning conversations, would have to engage in the dialogue of learning, I chose to stay with sisters. Stay mute. My grammar school experience, even with a different religious order, taught me that sisters operated in a more didactic style, allowing me to hide with the class herd, only speaking when called on.

Another consideration was money: B. C. High cost three times as much as Cathedral.

I was working nearly a full time job, earning enough not only to cover the annual high school tuition of $55, clothing, and spending money, but also giving my mother money for my sisters' needs. The after-school job meant that I rushed out of school every afternoon to get downtown before three, obviating any extra-curricular activities, or just hanging out with other students. I had made a few friends, but no one really close, not like in grammar school.

How much talking do you have to do in drafting? I asked myself. I was convincing myself that it would be a good idea to change schools, to go to Boston Technical High School and study drafting so I could get a better job, one like Ronnie's sister's boy friend. I was enrolled in the general course, taking typing and other clerical subjects in addition to a basic high school curriculum. College was not in my sights. College is for those kids on the trolley from City Point, Ronnie had told me. Not for us.

In order to get my transcript from Cathedral, I had to bring a parent to school to see Sister Honoria, the principal.

Problem was that both parents were working, and it was not possible to get them to take a day off from work to help their son sort out his educational future.

Why of course! I'll take my favorite nephew to change schools, exuded Aunt Madeline. What time?

Zita's baby sister had heard about my dilemma and offered to take me to Cathedral to see the principal, and then drive me over to Tech. Being her only sister's son, the sister who brought her up, being named the same name as her own son who died in infancy, Madeline always seemed partial to me. Madeline was eleven years younger than Zita, she was a much more stylish dresser -- at that time she was an artificially enhanced blonde -- and she didn't stutter. She also drove.

So, one bright day, we pulled up to school in a shiny black Pontiac, the one that her husband, Uncle Eddie, an MBTA starter, used when he moonlighted on funerals. We swooped in, Madeline wearing a fox stole over a dark suit, and went right to the principal's office.

Good afternoon, Sister, Madeline said presenting herself as my mother. We're so grateful to you and the other sisters for the fine school you have here at Cathedral High. This young man has really grown so much here. And, his father and I have been very impressed with the quality of religious instruction that is such an important part of your curriculum. Thank you so much, Sister. Now, the reason we are here is that it is our belief that he will greatly benefit from learning drafting. So far, Sister Superior had not moved a muscle. Unfortunately, Sister, that is a subject not available here. We are very sad to say, therefore, that the best course for the child is to transfer to a school that can offer that. For his future, you see. Regrettably.

I can see you have given this a great deal of thought. What school do you have in mind? the principal asked, examining her own fingernails.

There was nothing to sign, Sister Honoria gave Madeline no problem at all.

I would only ask that you are really sure about this move, she said, filling out the transfer form. I can tell you that it is always easier to leave than it is to come back. We have only so many seats here. In the public system, they have to take any child who comes to them. We do not. Cathedral High is very much in demand. Occasionally, we do have a student who leaves early to go into the military -- although we strongly prefer that they graduate first – but I cannot recall the last student who left to go to a public school.

Sister, I cannot thank you enough for your help and your consideration. May I ask that you remember us in your prayers, Aunt Madeline, taking charge, closed the meeting as she put the transcript in her purse.

Thank you, Sister, good bye, I piped up.

Next stop, Boston Technical High School. The instant we got in the door of the public school, Madeline began wrinkling her nose and frowning. The halls were not clean and neat as was Cathedral High. No shiny waxed floors. No religious pictures and statues. No girls. The boys were dressed as if they were hanging on the street corner.

They don't look like serious students, said she as she led me by the elbow through the corridor. I don't like the location of this school, your Uncle Eddie tells me that this is not a good area, she whispered.

Look at that," Madeline said peeking in on a class in session. "That teacher is shoving that boy up against the wall. I don't know about this place.

The black Pontiac reversed its route, back to Union Park Street – Cathedral High.

Look, let me go in to see Sister Honoria alone, Madeline said, setting the parking brake.

After what seemed a long time, I was called in.

The important thing about making mistakes in this life, my boy, said Sister Honoria, is what we learn and how we correct them. Like Our Lord's parable of the seeds, you have heard the truth, and therefore you will grow. Congratulations. I'm sure Sister Catania can fit you into your old courses. Now, pay attention to me. If it is that you really want to do this drafting business, here's what you can do. *Graduate.* Get your diploma from Cathedral High, you'll never be sorry. Then, you can take a night course in drafting – or whatever -- after graduation. That way, you'll have your education and you can get your drafting too.

The next vocational quandary came a few months later when I was convinced that I wanted to follow the kid before me at my after-school job and join the Franciscans. I signed up for extra Latin courses and began to talk to my teachers about the idea.

Very difficult choice, my home room sister said. No seminary will take a boy who stutters. Especially a junior seminary. Remember, she said, they have their pick of boys. Not even the Franciscans would let you in. They're looking for healthy boys.

Is there anything I can do in religious life? I asked.

If you want to wait until after you've graduated from high school – and you have really good grades, especially in Latin and Religion – perhaps . . . perhaps you could try some of the contemplative groups, like the Benedictines, maybe even the Trappists.

I was devastated. Jam was the last thing I wanted to make. A cloistered life of silence, meditation and perpetual introspection seemed to me to be running away from the world, hiding from the responsibility to make of one's life a contribution. I felt in a quandary, purposeless. Even if there had been someone at home to talk to, between school and work, I was never there.

Here you are, on the ground floor of a new business, Alan Levy argued, well liked, you should take advantage of what you have, and learn the business while you're working here. As I began to ask around about other career possibilities, I had approached the new MBA in the office where I worked after school. Levy talked about the investment business, mutual funds in particular.

I dunno, I balked. What I really want is to do something that means something to . . . other people, something that helps people -- but also that pays enough to get by.

Ike was in the White House, and Alan Levy was all for trickle-down economic theory. You have to remember that investments – when people buy stocks, say – that money flows to corporations, businesses like, say, Raytheon. They hire people in order to produce their product. Those people then have the money to raise families, to have a life.

Plausible, I thought, but I still was not enthralled with the idea of spending my whole life in an office like the one I was working in. Plus, I didn't know of anyone from South Boston who worked for Raytheon.

One of the advantages of a central high school was that you got to meet kids you would not have known otherwise. People who lived in other parts of the city, who came from different home situations, and who had perhaps a more expanded world view.

Sometime in the sophomore year I became friendly with a student who traveled to the South End from Dorchester's Savin Hill section. We sat through most classes together, had similar interests, and often shared the walk along the stretch of Washington Street from school to the Dover Street El station. We also shared being the butt of high school jokes. Me, because I was fat and stammered, Dominic because he was very thin and had some fruity mannerisms.

Dominic's father was an Italian immigrant who had built a very successful business. His mother's path to the U.S. included a childhood in Uruguay after leaving Italy just before Mussolini came to power.

The youngest of four, Dominic had an older sister in the convent, and another headed that way. His brother was at Holy Cross. The mother was an educated woman who helped in the office of the family business around the corner from the house. Household help gave her time to produce delectable Italian foods in her huge kitchen. Because this was a family that took education very seriously, it was unclear why Dominic was not following his brother at B.C. High.

They lived in a large Victorian house with a generous old barn that housed some of the business and family vehicles. Dominic's family were pillars of St.William's parish, he and his sisters also participated in every musical variety show that the active community put on. They maintained a summer home at Goose Rocks Beach, Kennebunkport, Maine.

Dominic had a driver's license and car virtually the instant he turned sixteen. He would often drive his brand-new Buick two-door, two-tone, big-finned roadster from Savin Hill to the Old Colony. Joe-Joe would be sitting reading the newspaper just inside the door when he knocked. Responding, Dominic, when asked, Joe-Joe would invite him to come through the unlocked door, and then gesture to the closed door of my room. After some talk about homework, we usually went out for a ride. Frequently on Saturday afternoons when I wasn't working, I would go along for the ride when Dominic drove out to Lexington for piano lessons.

It may have been that the friendship was built partly on my attraction to Dominic's family and the stability they represented. The kitchen and all within it was certainly not a deficit, either, nor were the Saturday vistas of the western suburbs. Two factors seem to have pushed the friendship to the background as the high school years went on: my increasing preoccupation with my after-school job and the world that came with it, and women. I was finally beginning to date.

Being an intelligent boy, overweight, a chronic stutterer, and working virtually full-time, obviated a social life as an adolescent. While I had puppy crushes on girls in the parallel classes at St. Augustine's since about the fourth grade, I had had no dates. There were the group boy/girl events to skating rinks and the like, but I had not had any significant, one-on-one girl contact until the junior year of high school. One of my few friends from school fixed me up with his sister. While she was not really my type, she did live in East Milton, a socio-economic spaceship ride away from the project, and I guess that was enough for me. An added bonus was that because she went to an upscale Catholic girls school, I thought I could meet other girls not from South Boston through her.

And I did.

Not long after we broke up, my friend's sister began to date another boy from our high school class who had dropped out to of school to join the navy. This boy had a relatively new automobile as well as a reputation for being quite a drinker. Late one night they were in a very serious accident. He survived, she did not. I wanted to express my condolences to the girl's family. I went to her house, something I had never done before. We usually met someplace else because her parents were not enthusiastic about our relationship. Finally, now that she was dead, I was at her house. It seemed like such a big place for one family. Even the land around it seemed more like a park than a house lot. Every window shade was pulled down in mid-day. No one answered the door when I rang.

If I hadn't dropped her, perhaps she'd still be alive, I thought. I felt responsible for her death. I still do.

It was clear that school was not a priority for me at this time. I was also beginning a period of intellectual awkwardness in accepting the tenets of Catholicism. I had stopped going to mass. At the end of the summer before senior year, I had decided not to go back to school. Work was enough, I thought. Besides, for $350 I had just bought a very pre-war automobile and was feeling quite independent. As disappointed as Zita would be, my parents were totally uninvolved in these kinds of decisions.

One of my friends from school – the brother of the girl killed in the car crash --talked me into going back in September, just for the first day to see some kids and show off the "new" car. I stayed, completed the year, and graduated in June. Cardinal Cushing handed out the diplomas at a ceremony at the Cathedral on a warm June Sunday afternoon. I felt relieved, but still purposeless.

Old South Building, 294 Washington Street, Boston.

Chapter Fourteen

Securities Company of Massachusetts was the underwriter for two relatively – by Boston standards -- new mutual funds.

I had no idea what they did. The only connection I could make with the term "underwriter" was the tag on electrical cords

– lamps, Christmas tree lights, etc. --that talked about Underwriters' Laboratory.

Financial institutions in my fourteen-year-old's world were savings banks and credit unions. The savings bank was the Greek temple on Broadway between the supermarket and the movie house. I never went in there, but knew some kids who collected dimes and quarters and pressed them into holes in cardboard books and brought them in there. During the war there was a large War Bond thermometer suspended between the columns over the front door.

Later on, I discovered the credit union in the Old Harbor project, just a few blocks over from where we lived, and I had a Christmas Club account there a few years in a row. My friend Ronnie had one, so I thought it was a pretty good idea. I was vaguely aware that my father had joined the Knights of Columbus so that he could borrow from their credit union to buy a car.

Since she graduated from high school, Zita had worked on and off for the same insurance company, taking time off to have and tend children, returning when the oldest started high school himself. I understood that insurance paid if you had a car and had an accident. Then there was life insurance. Barbara Stanwyck explained all about that in "Double Indemnity."

Closer to home, there was the John Hancock man.

For all the years our family lived in the project, an "insurance man" came to the door to collect $1.52 weekly premium. One of Joe-Joe's prized possessions was a mahogany Governor Winthrop style slat-front desk from Paine's Furniture Company. It sat just inside the front door. (The only door.) Opening the slat front, which doubled as a writing surface never used as such, the desk had many pigeonholes, four little drawers and a tabernacle-like compartment flanked by two secret compartments. The insurance book and premium money, always in exact change, were kept in one of these compartments. Suit and tie, the man came to the door every week. Whoever answered the door when he knocked, gave him the book and the money. He took the money, made a note in the book and returned it – until next week.

Anyone in the family who borrowed the insurance money was under pain of interdict to return it before Tuesday when Mr. John Hancock came around.

Project kids were totally unaware of the stock market and what it did. Certainly, the sisters never discussed it in school. The world of investments, stocks, bonds, coupon-clipping, was a universe outside our knowledge. There was awareness of the market crash, and people losing all their money, leading up to the Depression. That, too, was learned from the movies. And, of course, our parents talked about the Depression and its difficulties. However, a world peopled with men and women rich enough to have investments to lose, seemed more of a fantasy than much of the rest of what was seen on the silver screen.

Having had a taste of the work experience as a Customs laborer, and the money that came with it the previous summer, I made up my mind to find a part-time job once I got acclimated to high school. Looking through the want ads in the newspaper, I found that something called Securities Company of Massachusetts was looking for an office boy. Part-time. Experience required.

When I saw the ad, my imagination conjured up a huge office like American Mutual, where my mother worked. The next day, right after school, still in Catholic high school uniform of jacket, shirt, and necktie, I found my way to the address. I was surprised to find a very small office – albeit in a large office building -- of no more than a dozen people.

All right, said the pretty blond woman at the front desk, sit over there and fill out this form. Miss Harrington will come and talk to you in a few minutes.

The form was actually a 5"x7" card asking for such basic information as name, address, and social security number. I had to get a social security number when I worked for Mr. O'Toole on the docks the summer past, so I was all set.

Squirming as I filled it out, I sat looking at the hundred-year-old prints of packet ship advertisements for the Boston to San Francisco passage. Sitting in one of the two wooden straight chairs near the door, I surveyed the rest of that part of the office. Three gray steel desks with linoleum-like tops sat neatly in a row, each having a typewriter well and a secretary to operate the machine in it. Convinced they were all surreptitiously looking at the applicant, I squirmed some more and rehearsed in my mind answers to prospective questions, fearful of disclosing my stammer.

I should have gone to the bathroom before leaving school, I scolded myself, my plump thighs twitching. I dismissed the idea of making a trip to the men's room. Just having to ask where it was would be a giveaway, canceling out any possibility of getting the job, I was convinced.

I grew more nervous as I recalled the time just a few weeks ago when I got caught on the bus going to school with urination pangs. I was late for school that day because I had to catch the next bus home and change.

Finally, after what seemed like a span of time as long as chemistry class, a nice smelling woman came up to me, and after reading my full name on the card, said That's a good name for South Boston. Hello, my name is Carol Harrington, come this way.

She motioned for me to sit at the side of her desk, which was at the back of the suite looking at an airshaft. A dozen steps away was an open door to a corner office with an oriental rug and a leather easy chair in addition to a wooden executive desk and guest chairs.

Well no, I have never worked as an office boy before. I am experienced in working, though, I told her, I worked on the docks last summer. Drilling bales of wool. Kindly, she asked about my knowledge of certain office machines, postal rates, and the geography of Downtown Boston, particularly the Financial District.

I was blank.

Perhaps we should look at the mail room and some of the office machines, Miss Harrington suggested. If you'd like to use the men's room while I make a phone call, I'll meet you in the mail room in a few minutes, she gestured in the direction of the assigned meeting place and told me where the men's room was.

It's probably none of my business but, can you tell me why you want this job? Miss Harrington had shown me the machinery and the mailing room, explaining its equipment. The mailing room had a foot-thick door that was left open – it was housed in a room-sized, walk-in safety vault. This is a small office and I don't have time to train someone new every few weeks. I need someone who is dependable. Also, are you sure you can juggle your schoolwork and a job like this? The hours and the responsibilities are going to grow with this company. You don't want to be in the position of sacrificing your education for a part-time job, do you?

When she became convinced of my intentions, she relaxed and said, “Well, look, I think you have some learning to do -- in terms of office machinery, among other things -- but you seem to be bright, and you should be able to get it . . . in time. As for errands Downtown, I can get you a map. I’ll also get a manual from the Post Office on rates and procedures. Bring in your working papers tomorrow. Can you start today?”

I later learned that the job was open because the kid before me was leaving to go into a Franciscan novitiate seminary. He was from East Boston, an older kid of 17, and the office crew seem to have liked him very much. *Perhaps coming from Cathedral High School was a plus for me,* I thought. I started to work there that first day I went in to apply, and stayed for seven years: four years of high school, a year floundering after graduation, and the first two years of college.

Some guys grow up on the playing field, some grow up in the military. This is where I grew up. In a start-up mutual funds company. I would not have gone to college if I hadn’t taken this job. It was not just the money: money I earned, and money the company gave me for that first semester. More important than the money was the close contact with another world and its people. The world outside the projects and the neighborhood was a wondrous revelation to me as I was struggling to grow from a fourteen-year-old boy into a young man.

I learned not only that there was a world outside my peninsula community, but also that there was a way to get there without spending a lifetime in the secure, but to my mind at the time, dishwater dull jobs with the City, State, Gas, Edison, or public transit.

People actually do live in houses like the ones in the movies, I told myself. *And the ones my parents used to take us to at Christmas time outside the city to look at the lights.*

Does anyone really live in these houses? Zita would wonder aloud as we drove through quiet suburban areas. I never see people around. No one inside these brand new picture windows. Where is everyone? Certainly not like the projects where kids are out in the streets and parents are sitting on steps.

The office was housed in the Old South Building, adjacent to historic Old South Church on Washington Street, abutting Newspaper Row. When I first saw the name of the building, I was confused. Disney's "Song of the South" was one of my favorite movies as a child. It was one of the many that my father took me to see in Boston's numerous movie palaces, thriving in the years right after the war. That was when we were still father and son. The combination live action and animation film featuring Br'er Rabbit, Br'er Bear, and Br'er Fox presented an excessively idyllic version of the Ante-Bellum South.

I couldn't understand why a building in downtown Boston would be named after the Old South.

It was the church, Old South Meeting House, that the building was named after, because it was built on its yard.

Organized in 1669, Old South Meeting House was the Sons of Liberty site for the organization of the Boston Tea Party. To punish the colonists for the rebellion, the British ripped out pulpit and pews, brought in horses, and used it for a riding school. Not long after the Civil War, fashionable Boston citizens were moving West, and the Meeting House congregation moved across the Common to Copley Square into a new Northern Italian Baroque building and called itself Old South Church. The original building was spared from demolition and a state-of-the art office building was erected on its churchyard in 1907.

Raymond's Department Store, Washington Street, Boston, 1957.

Raymond's department store, "Where U Bot the Hat," was the natural extremity of retail Washington Street in the 1950s. Old South was the next block. Across the street was a

Nedick's hot dog emporium, and then there was Newspaper Row. The Globe had not yet moved to Dorchester, but the Herald Traveler had moved down to Avery and Mason Streets, closer to the Combat Zone. Both the Boston Post and the Record American were still in business. Housed in ancient, narrow red brick buildings, the papers' front windows had large blackboards with the latest headlines posted. This was the older part of town, with many narrow thoroughfares like Pi Alley, so named for the falling lead type from newspaper composing rooms. Water Street, a mere alley on one side of the Old South Bulding connecting Devonshire with Washington streets is not much wider than a Volkswagen is long.

At midcentury, upper Washington Street combined the bustle of the retail district, with the drama of the newspaper business, and the overlay of smart-looking people going to and from their jobs in nearby office buildings. The pushcart market area, with the North End beyond, lie only a few blocks away. City Hall, a few steps from the legendary Parker House, was just up School Street. Coming in town from the project on the streetcar and the subway, walking past the big department stores, entering the three-stories tall cream and white marble lobby of the Old South Building, was an impressive moment. This was not a church, not a museum, not even a hotel. This was a place where people got dressed up to come to work.

In the world of the projects, as hard-working as the neighbors were in those days, very few got dressed up to go to work. If the sisters had any vocational goals for their South Boston charges, it was to prepare us for jobs for which we had to dress up. A few men from the project – my father and Mishy's included -- wore suits and ties getting on the bus, but most were in work clothes like the men I had worked with on the docks the previous summer. Some of the working mothers worked in offices and they dressed up. This was that kind of world. Not much more than two miles away from the projects, Boston's emerging financial district in the 1950s was light years away.

There were two budget-genteel restaurants in the building: Slagle's for breakfast and lunch, and Huyler's for lunch only; a dry cleaners, barber shop, shoe shine stand, and cobbler on the lower level, and, of course, a newsstand in the massive lobby itself. The "Hole in the Wall" take-out coffee and sandwich shop was in the alley outside the Water Street door. There was also an entrance on Milk Street, number 10. Most of the major railroads had offices in the building, for whatever reason; it wasn't especially close to South Station, the nearest depot. Lawyers and accounting firms filled the other offices in the eight-story sand-colored brick building. Securities Company of Massachusetts was the only investment company. Most investment houses were on State Street, a few blocks away.

Investment Trust of Boston and Income Fund of Boston were early mutual funds. Little more than a quarter century before, the first U.S. mutual fund, Massachusetts Investors Trust, made financial history by jumping from $50,000 in assets to a massive $320,000 in its first year, 1924. The Stock Market crash and the formation of the Securities and Exchange Commission, combined with the Depression, slowed development of the mutual fund.

World War II had been over for six years when I first set foot in Securities Company of Massachusetts. Mutual funds, I was told, were the wave of the future for the small investor. It was a way to pool investments and the cost of managing them so that even ordinary middle class people could get into the market. As the country was recovering from the war-interrupted domestic economic stagnation, there was renewed interest in mutual funds as an investment vehicle for the wealth beginning to accumulate.

Joe-Joe always told me that we were middle class, but I didn't see much of that accumulating wealth where we lived.

My primary job was to wrap and mail thousands of prospectuses and other interpretive/promotional material to brokers. Wilshire Boulevard and Collins Avenue addresses sparked my imagination. There were also many in Texas, the mid-Atlantic region, as well as the Chicago area. I ran errands, fetched coffee, and was responsible for the office machinery. Perhaps the most temperamental office contraption of the day was the Apeco copy machine. In 1951 carbon paper was still used for routine business correspondence, but photostatic copies were the cutting edge for special documents, especially those with signatures. It was a wet method, the fluid having to be changed regularly, and it produced two sheets of paper – negative and positive – that came out very damp and glued together. The trick was to pull them apart at just the right stage of doneness.

As the years went on, other duties came my way, including a stint at cleaning the boss's apartment in Copley Square, and helping a polio-stricken manager with some of his personal functions.

The owner was a Texan and a Jew. Both were strikes against him in the Boston investment world at that time. He worked overtime to minimize both strikes. It was hard. By this time the Irish dominated Boston, but Yankees owned it. Banks, insurance companies, newspapers were all in the hands of old Protestant families. The inner core of Boston financial circles at that time was Harvard, while the founder of Securities Company of Massachusetts was Rice Institute. They were Union Club,

Algonquin Club, Somerset Club, while he was YMCU gym. They were Unitarian and Episcopalian, he worked hard to hide his Jewish heritage.

Somehow he was able to recruit a complement of Brahmins to fill the Advisory Board. It didn't hurt that he had been a major in the army, and had seen action in the European theater. With a full, Teddy Roosevelt mustache, and made-to-measure ultra-conservative suits draped over erect military bearing, the financier packaged himself as his vision of what a Yankee businessman would look, act, and sound like at mid-century, which in Boston looked very much like that of the World War I era.

Unmarried, his business -- and the cultivation of a Proper Bostonian persona – was his life. Business connections, he soon learned, with some of the Yankee hoi polloi did not transfer to social invitations. While he often invited them to vacation with him in the Bahamas, they never seem to have invited him to lunch, let alone dinner or an evening at Symphony.

This was a time in which religion, class, and social background were more relevant in the Boston business universe than education. And it lingered on. Only a dozen years after that time, returning to Boston after active duty in the navy and looking for a job to utilize my bachelor's degree in English, I was told by the senior Vice President of a major Boston-based textbook publisher that while they were very interested in hiring me, I should understand that Catholics could never enter into the management track in the company. Editorial and art positions were open to me, but not management. So did I want the job or not?

This was just how it was. It was consistent with banking, insurance, and other major sectors of Boston's business community at mid-century. Certain families, colleges, and prep schools were feeders to the important positions in Boston. While many families kept "places" on the Hill or in the Back Bay, most had long since moved outside the city to northern or western suburbs. Politically, they exerted control through "The Vault," an informal business advisory body to the mayor. Very rarely, with exception-proving-the-rule examples like Oliver Ames running for State Representative from the Back Bay as late as 1961, did they get directly involved. WASPs controlled the cultural institutions such as Boston Symphony Orchestra, Museum of Fine Arts, the Athenaeum, and of course, Massachusetts General Hospital, and they were very interested in the various historical associations – the past – but their disdain for the living city was palpable.

Anyone outside their group just didn't count. Catholics in general, but Irish and Italians particularly, as well as Jews, were beyond the pale. Blacks and Hispanics hadn't happened yet.

Joseph David Ernst was fiercely workaholic, a perfectionist who expected everyone around him to be as zealous as was he. That included his mailroom staff: the office boy. This first job became the prototype for others in my life. Kind of a PT 109 model. Command of albeit a smaller entity, but, yet, clear and total responsibility for a defined area of activity, and clearly measurable outcomes and results. Because I came to work after school, getting there sometime between two and three in the afternoon, I was still working when it came to be five o'clock and people started putting on their hats. Normally I was not through until 6 at the earliest. It was a company rule to get material in the mail the same day the request was received. The parcel post window at the post office a couple of blocks away at Congress and Milk streets, closed at 6:30. I was given a key to the office, and closed up when I was finished. I was there most Saturdays at least through early afternoon.

On perhaps 4-5 occasions each month when the market ran late, or something else would keep other staffers, Mr. Ernst would take everyone who was left in the office out to dinner. Including “the kid.” He had four favorite spots: Newbury Steak House near Massachusetts and Commonwealth Avenues, La Cantina still today on Hanover Street in the North End, Harpoot’s, Middle Eastern restaurant in the South End, and a nameless Chinese restaurant on Hudson Street.

It was quite an experience for a kid from the projects. Once in a great while, my family would stop at a cafeteria or diner style restaurant when out in the car driving around on a Sunday. But, other than the time my maternal grandfather introduced me to octopus at the European Restaurant, I had not been to an eatery with table service. More important than the food was the association with the office staff in a non-business setting. It seemed exhilarating to be going to restaurants with a group of smart adults, well-dressed in their suits and ties and women’s business dresses. The colors of the nighttime city, the scent of exotic food, the sophisticated dinner partners, made lasting impressions on the boy from East Ninth Street.

Mr. Ernst’s secretary, Carol Harrington, who hired me, often worked late too. She was young, divorced and had a crush on her boss. She seemed very, very good at what she did. Mr. Ernst was a superb salesman and big-picture person, but not overly interested in the details of running a business. Carol was a detail-focused natural manager. She ran the operations of the business for years, until he hired a hotshot – male – Harvard MBA from New York. Fairly often when her boy friend came to the office late to pick her up, and the office boy was still there, they would take me with them for drinks. Of course, nonalcoholic for the youngster. Occasionally, I would also have dinner with them. Carol liked the Rib Room in the Hotel Somerset, the Red Coach Grill on Stanhope Street, and anyplace in the Copley Plaza – technically, the Sheraton Plaza at this time.

The first time I remember feeling poor was one summer early in my time at Securities Company of Massachusetts when the office crew had a beach party. Stan, the investment analyst, was driving the car that picked me up at home that Saturday. There were three people in the car besides Stan when I got in.

The looks on their faces as they surveyed the street filled with identical, prison-like brick buildings, clothes hanging out to dry, children shrieking, all the other sights and sounds of a housing project in summertime, caused me to almost feel their pity.

This incident bothered me more than the taunts of the neighborhood toughs, the hellfire and brimstone cosmogony of the sisters, the future-less lives of too many of my classmates from grammar school, and the overall grittiness of life.

A quiet street in Beacon Hill.

Chapter Fifteen

Boston's Beacon Hill neighborhood is known for its Federalist row houses, narrow cobbled-stone streets, wrought-iron street lights, and brick sidewalks. However, if it were not for Mahatma Gandhi, the signature sidewalks would have long ago been torn up and replaced with concrete like the rest of the city.

In the immediate post-War years, Gandhi was in the news as Great Britain was readying to grant Indian independence in 1947. Joe-Joe attained his goal of a City job not long after the war was over. Knowing that the City was gearing up to address some long-deferred roadwork, he studied engineering aspects of road-building and passed a Civil Service exam, joined the Paving Division and became an inspector. It was there that he – and Mayor James Michael Curley, expert politician that he was -- encountered the legacy of the Indian leader.

It was also in this period that, through my father's assignments in various parts of the city that I became aware of its size and diversity. Appalled by what they saw as the blight brought upon their beautiful city by hordes of new Irish immigrants, older Brahmin families began to relocate from Boston to areas north and west of the city shortly after the turn of the century. Nevertheless, at midcentury, Beacon Hill was still the seat of the Brahmin-Yankee establishment, and therefore Boston's wealthiest section. Mayor Curley was in the midst of a sweeping plan to remake the face of Boston before the mid-century mark. Part of this plan involved tearing up all of Boston's trademark brick sidewalks and replacing them with artificial stone, otherwise known as cement. More even, safer, and the replacement process employed a lot of people.

This was fine with most Bostonians, who were eager to get into the twentieth century. Problem was that the people in Beacon Hill weren't with the program. They didn't mind the eighteenth century and loved their brick sidewalks, thank you, uneven and unsafe as they were. Tradition was their thing. Ceding control – with abundant legislative checks and balances -- of the administrative machinery of municipal government to these Celtic newcomers was one thing, but letting them dictate the streetscape of their fortress neighborhood was quite another.

What next? Giving up their purple window glass for picture windows?

Beacon Hill citizenry rallied 'round, held meetings, circulated petitions, wrote letters to the editor, in general, made a lot of noise. They wanted their brick sidewalks to stay. Curley wanted them gone. After exhausting every other avenue, the civic association went political. Representatives in the State House and City Hall pulled out every stop, including a meeting with the Mayor, who their district had unfailingly opposed in every election.

Knowing he had nothing to lose, Curley did not back down, didn't even offer a compromise. Instead, he lectured them for being more concerned about the antiquarian appearances of their area than the safety of their elderly neighbors, many of whom lived in the remaining rooming houses – and did support him.

The civic association decided to take drastic action. They were going to put their women on the line. Mahatma Gandhi was about the only one in the newsreels shown practicing conscientious objection at that time. Perhaps the ladies of Beacon Hill were inspired. If a skinny little Indian in a diaper could defeat the power of the British Empire, they reasoned, a group of determined Beacon Hill ladies could certainly take the wind out of the not-quite-yet Last Hurrah.

The first morning that the City Paving Division trucks showed up on Beacon Hill, a delegation of dowagers was there to meet them. Earlier they had fished out the folding chairs that they used to take to Esplanade concerts, put them out on the sacred bricks making up the sidewalk, sat down with their needlework and their "Town and Country" magazines and sat there as self-assured as if they were behind the house in their enclosed garden. When the foreman had mustered up enough strength to deferentially ask them – *if they wouldn't mind, ma'ams* -- to please get up so the men could begin their sacrilegious work, the ladies, returning the civility, refused to move.

The foreman made trips down to Charles Street to the closest drug store to call City Hall for advice.

Several trips.

Just before lunch break, the workmen jumped up in the trucks and rumbled away.

The following days demonstrated the heightened level of organization of the Ladies of the Sidewalk. As the City tried to outfox them by not announcing in advance the name of the street that would be first, the Ladies did the outfoxing by having units of their force ready to come out of their houses at the first sight of a City truck. The nimble Ladies were out on the bricks before the workmen hopped out of their trucks. Didn't matter which part of the Hill, the Ladies had it covered with the synchronization of a ballet corps.

Clearly, the Beacon Hill Ladies won this one. Curley's people had to move on to more docile neighborhoods like Dorchester, South Boston, Roslindale, and the North and West Ends. How many of the Ladies husbands would have wanted jobs in the Paving Department of the City, anyway?

The Hill liked their brick sidewalks so much that their women staged a sit-in to keep them. Years later other neighborhoods stood in line to ditch the ugly concrete sidewalks for brick. Who knows what would have happened if more neighborhoods heeded the teachings of Gandhi?

"International Conflict in an American City: Boston's Irish, Italians, and Jews, 1935-1944," John F. Stack, Jr., Greenwood Press, Westport, Conn., 1979

Pre-World War II playground and refreshment stand at Castle Island.

Chapter Sixteen

After Nana there were the sisters. Then there was Carol. Then Phyllis. And Marie. More than men, it seems that women -- older women -- had a formative influence on me.

Since requests for prospectus usually are a bit lighter in summer, that means I don't have to deal with the 6:30 curfew of the parcel post window, I said to Carol the week after graduation from high school.

Yeah, that's right.

So, do you think I could probably close up here by 5:30 during the summer?

Probably. Why do you ask?

Well, look, Carol, I've been thinking about ways to make some extra money for whatever flavor of schooling I wind up doing, and I've been looking at a second job – just for the summer.

Another job? Carol put down the papers she was proofing and gave the office boy her full attention. Can you handle two jobs? Even if it is only for a couple of months?

I think so. There is a night shift job at the Howard Johnson's over on the Common."

Right beside Loew's Theatre, she interjected. Good hot fudge.

Yes. That's about a ten-minute walk. The shift starts at six. They say they get a supper crowd and then another rush after the movies let out. If I came in here in the morning to get all the office machinery problems and errands out of the way before starting mailing after lunch, I should be able to leave by 5:30, don't you think?

When I got no response, Carol?

Look, how long is this night shift, anyway?

I'd go on at 6:00. They close at 11:00. There is some clean-up, so it's between five and six hours.

Every night? his boss asked.

Five nights. Mondays and Tuesdays I'd be off.

You run about 35-40 hours here in the summer, and you're talking about adding another 30 hours? Doubling your work time? she asked raising her unplucked eyebrows. I know you're young, but it does sound like a lot. You know, I've done those counter jobs as a kid. It's no picnic being on your feet for 5-6 hours at a stretch. After being on them all day here.

I had nothing to say. She got up from her desk and looked out her window into the air shaft still bright in the late spring sun after 5:00. Well, she exhaled, you're sure you want to do this?

I do. I'm not doing anything else. And, one way or another – night school or day school – I am going to need the money.

And another thing, Carol said, reclaiming her seat, wouldn't hurt being around people your own age, either! Okay, look, I don't have a problem with this, and I don't think Mr. Ernst will. I'll talk to him in the morning.

A few years older than me, Phyllis lived with her father and brother in City Point. She was a senior at Emmanuel College, which was staffed by the same order of sisters that ran St. Augustine's School. She read Nietzche, Beckett, Sartre, Dostoevsky and Kant and wore her agnosticism on her sleeve. This emancipated 50's woman worked the same shift at Howard Johnson's that summer I did.

After closing up we would walk over to Kneeland Street to catch the Bay View bus home, she staying on when I got off at the project. While she was a very good friend, our relationship was that of an older, world-weary, intellectual sister and her bright but naïve baby brother. At least, that's how Phyllis saw it. Discovering that my Cathedral High education had some gaps, she – who had gone to Girls' Latin -- quickly introduced me to the existential philosophers and other heroes of 1950s intellectual wannabes.

I brought you another stack, Phyllis said, putting on her apron as she punched in. She handed me a brown paper bag filled with books. Take as long as you want. You've got a lot of catching up to do.

Thanks. Uh, I'm not sure I got all Nietzche was talking about.

We can get a cup of coffee at the Waldorf near the bus stop after work, if you want?

We also had supper a few times before the shift. Part of Phyllis's curriculum was current cinema; at least a few times that summer we went to see a foreign film in one of the art houses around town.

While Carol and Alan Levy talked up college as a way to get ahead in the world materially, Phyllis's incentives were the development of the life of the mind. As much as she urged me to get a university education at all costs, Phyllis was short on specifics.

It was Carol Harrington who told me all about night college classes and how they worked.

You can take business courses one at a time, and eventually get a college degree. Eight years, ten years. Goes by pretty fast. Now, I'm taking a course in accounting that starts in September.

Accounting? I asked.

Absolutely. It is essential. I've taken five courses already, may even major in accounting. You're going to need it.

I am?

Yep, said she as she snapped her steno book shut. We can ride over to BU together after work.

But how do I . . .

She explained all about registration, how to choose courses, what to expect in the classroom. It's not like high school, you know. No one looks out for you, no one tells you what to do, you have to do your own navigation, she told me.

I thought about it. This second string approach appealed to me. Zita told me that's what her brother John did. While I was not aware of it at the time, it tied in with my choice of high schools. I had been able to conceal my stutter by avoiding class participation, avoiding talking much at all. In that I worked, and there was no time for any social life in high school, I came and went with as little interaction as possible. I was so disconnected that when senior prom time came around, for example, I had no thoughts of going until one of the women in the office pressured me to take her younger sister. All the way over to Medford. She was cute as a button, but had a steady boy friend who was in the army. We went, had a great time. Period.

Back to academics. I was bright enough to handle the course material without relying on insights from the classroom. Thinking about college, however, I reflexively dismissed my own ability to survive in a milieu of bright, young and articulate college students. The night school anonymity of larger classes and struggling adults appealed to me both academically and socially.

Carol went with me for that first registration. I was expecting a formal process like a swearing in. What I saw was an auditorium filled with tables of paper and punch cards. We waited in line with throngs of others, filled out forms, walked up Commonwealth Avenue to the Bursar's Office to pay. And so began my collegiate career with two courses. First semester was Principles of Accounting on Tuesday and Thursday evenings, and Introduction to Economics on Mondays and Wednesday.

It was a slog, working full time, studying part-time, and going to class four nights a week. By the beginning of the second semester I was beginning to think that perhaps I was not cut out for the business courses. It was not just the material, I enjoyed the economics course. It was more where it led. The other students seemed so materialistic, so grubby in a distasteful way. I didn't want to become them. Apparently, Phyllis had turned me into an intellectual in waiting. I was convinced that, as desperate as I was to get out of the housing project level of living, there had to be something else in life than just earning the money to do so.

Mr. Ernst heard about all this. He heard about everything in his company. At the conclusion of the second semester of night school, he called me in to his sunny corner office one afternoon for a talk. He was probing to see if I wanted to go to college – to day school -- and what I wanted to study. Learn something practical, son, he said, echoing Joe-Joe.

When Mr. Ernst began to get the idea that his office boy might want to study liberal arts, he warned against becoming a dilettante. In his ersatz Boston Brahmin tough-guy, skinflint persona, he wanted to help. He told me that if I decided that I wanted to start college, I could count on the company to help. Of course, he explained, my father would be expected to help, and I should plan on using my savings. The bottom line was that he would give me my Christmas bonus early, in September, if I chose to go to day school.

A semester's tuition at Boston University in 1956 was less than $400. The office boy's expected Christmas bonus was around $300. Housing was not an issue, I was living at home. My continued tenure with Securities Company was guaranteed.

That would pay for books and incidentals, while still continuing to help my parents financially.

I was home free.

I told Mr. Ernst I would think about it.

I hadn't the foggiest idea what I wanted to do.

I had the summer to figure it out.

Probably because she ate out so much, and hung around so many different hotels, Carol knew someone who was the chief bellman at the Oceanside Hotel in Magnolia, Massachusetts, just outside Gloucester. Or, it could have been that he was a friend of her late father's. Like him, this guy worked the circuit. Florida in the winter time, New England in summer. This was his fifth year in Magnolia and he was hiring a staff for the summer – mostly college kids and a sprinkling of hotel pros -- and he needed a Beach Club Driver, someone to drive the guests the quarter of a mile from the hotel to the private beach.

The hotel itself sat on a steep rocky promontory with sweeping views of the ocean, but had no direct beachfront. Only a thin strip of muddy sand and huge rocks at low tide known as Cobblestone Beach. It was built long before people went on vacation primarily to sun and swim. During the War when the current owners bought it, they also bought an oceanfront lot around the corner on Bathing Beach. On it they built a simple concrete-block building, that looked like an oversized garage, to house changing areas, a makeshift snack bar, and a service bar. They called it Oceanside Beach Club, it was open only to Oceanside Hotel guests and those locals who took out a membership.

It was the spring of 1956 that Carol had obviously noticed that her office boy was near burnout. She told me that if I was interested, she would hire another kid to take my place and work the summer months only as office boy for Securities Company of Massachusetts, letting me take a summer job in Magnolia and come back to my old job at the office after Labor Day. In time to register as a freshman day student at BU.

Deal.

Gloucester's heroic harborside statue, "Man at the Wheel" is more than the logo of a fish company, it is a memorial to the more than 10,000 Gloucestermen claimed by the sea. A gritty port city of about 30,000, located 30 miles north of Boston, long the cynosure of fishermen and attendant industries, Gloucester bills itself as America's oldest seaport. Gloucester was a thriving shipbuilding center in the early 18th century, and had been a thriving fishing port in the 18th and 19th centuries, and well into the early part of the 20th. Gorton-Pew Fisheries, perhaps the port's iconic industry, morphed into Gorton's of Gloucester, purveyor of fish sticks and other mass-market seafood. By mid-20th century, however, in spite of the influx of Italian and Portuguese fishermen, Gloucester was no longer a beehive of commerce, but had begun the slide toward seediness.

Beginning with native son Fitz Hugh Lane, Gloucester was known as an art center as early as 50 years after the American Revolution. Winslow Homer, Childe Hassam, and Edward Hopper were but a few of the many American painters drawn to the natural splendor of the area. The Rocky Neck section boasts the oldest artist colony in the U.S. It was so popular that cruise liners stopped there regularly in the summer months, providing fuel to the art market. Although by 1956, its position as an arts center had long since been eclipsed by

Provincetown, the size and variety of the Gloucester artists community continued to convey a certain cachet. Gloucester's main street, however, still had more thrift shops and second-hand furniture stores than galleries or even the next stage, souvenir emporia.

Magnolia was a kind of boutique section of Cape Ann. It was on the water, and had many nineteenth century resort hotels, wood-frame Victorian behemoths with deep porches and colorful awnings. One of which, Magnolia Manor, had achieved regional celebrity as a "milk farm," or rehab spa for overweight ladies of a certain economic status. The premier spot in town, the 300-plus-room Oceanside Hotel and its cottages, pool, and tennis courts sprawled over blocks of spectacular oceanfront real estate. Like its vicinity sisters, Oceanside saw its heyday with a Yankee clientele in the years between the end of the Civil War and the beginning of World War I.

When I first saw it hunkering on the rocks overlooking the cold Atlantic in late May 1956, its wooden clapboards were still painted white, its deep porches still filled with an armada of rocking chairs.

It was now a Jewish house. Families would come from New York and Philadelphia to spend a month by the sea in Massachusetts. At least the women folk. Many of the breadwinners would work all week and come up on the Friday night train. The observant ones tried to get there in time for the Shabat Service held in the Grand Ballroom.

Seventh Avenue garment-district style racks of clothing would be unloaded from the train; some came by car. It was not unusual for families to rent an additional room just to house their costume changes. They came to look at the sea, to be seen, to pretend to learn to play tennis, to eat, to dance the cha-cha and the tango. There was a little cocktail lounge, the Rose

Room, where the wise guys hung out. There were fashion shows and dancing lessons by the pool. Probably much the same activities the Yankees enjoyed when they were the dominant patrons.

It was a muted Catskills. And I loved it at first sight. Even better than Condon's Farm, because I got paid.

I got there just before the season started, and worked on the switchboard until the rest of the staff arrived. A Greek fraternal group, American Hellenic Educational Progressive Association -- AHEPA -- had rented most of the hotel in early June for their annual convention. The first night of their stay I answered a call that blew my sister school sensibilities.

Hey, uh, Pallie, can you help us liven things up a bit? a raspy voice queried.

How can I help you, sir? said I.

Well, for starters, we need some girls up here. Know what I mean?

I'm sorry. Housekeeping doesn't have anyone available until morning.

Hey, kid, are you kidding? We're not interested in cleaning ladies. How do we get some *fun* girls, know what I mean? he tried again.

Uh . . . not sure . . .

Hey kid, do I have to spell it out? Call girls! Prostitutes! Hookers! Ladies of the Evening! Whatever you fishermen up here call them, we want some action.

Oh. I see.

Now that you see, Pallie, how soon can you get some action up here? I mean, you do want to keep your guests happy, don't you?

Also on site weeks before the season started was Roy, the pool "boy." Roy was a Cuban in his late twenties whose job it was to keep the cabanas stocked with towels and toiletries, to allot beach chairs, umbrellas, and towels at the pool itself, and to flirt with the female guests. Wiry build, not tall, Roy had augmented red hair and a permanent tan. Roy didn't live in the dormitories like the college kids, he had his own suite in one of the cabanas. Apparently this smooth operator was desperate for something to do one evening when he invited me and another guy who had also just arrived to his place to see a slide show of mosquitoes. You read that correctly.

Now, the new drink in Miami and in the best hotels in Havana is gin. Yes, gin. Surprised? he asked his guests.

What's new about gin? asked the other guy. Gin and tonic, martinis, Tom Collins?

Ah, but I'm talking about straight gin. Gin. The English say *neat*. Maybe with some ice. Rocks. Roy said as he dug some cubes out of a cooler and poured gin over them. Here, try this. This is not your auntie's Tom Collins.

After conversation – led by Roy – about the differences between night life in Havana and that in Miami, during which second drinks were poured, the talk got back to the purpose of the gathering.

Once his guests were settled sitting on the floor grasping their third drinks, Roy started the slides, giving a running commentary.

Did you know that mosquitoes are bisexual, he asked the two boys, both in our late teens, when an image came on that looked as though the two insects were embracing. That means that sex happens between males and females, and between males and males, and between females and females. Usually the case in nature, you know. Quite natural.

How do you know where the organs are? the other guy asked.

They can tell, replied the Cuban.

When an image was presented of three or four mosquitoes embracing, he continued his lecture, Now, group sex – you know, sex with more than two – is also very common in nature.

Looks as though they're all just kind of piled up together, I said, what's happening?

Roy then began a detailed description of homosexual sex among three – not mosquitoes, but human males – as he edged from his place near the projector to the floor where the boys were. His guests got nervous, got up and left -- with their gin – saying something about early morning assignments.

As the rest of the staff drifted in during the last week of June, it became apparent that the boy from South Boston was not alone in his lack of command of Yiddish. More than half of the staff was not Jewish. Brand-new Brandeis was represented by a brother-sister duo, Emmanuel had three, Regis two, there was one from UPenn, and one from what was then Salem Teacher's College, a trio from Cornell, and then others from schools that just didn't ring a bell with me.

However, I was the only college-age staffer who didn't have at least the freshman year at my back, and who had not previously lived away from home. As the summer went on, it dawned on me that Carol's motivation in hooking me up with this college orientation summer was to dispel feelings of inferiority, and to teach me how to socialize with the kind of kids who would be my academic peers – and competition. Both Carol and I knew intuitively that youth can sometimes mask poverty. I was bright, well-read, under Phyllis's tutelage I had become acquainted with the hot ideas of the day, and by the end of the summer I had learned to package myself in the prevailing collegiate ways of dressing.

I astounded myself. I fit in.

Except for the tennis pro and the beach boy, the staff lived in gender-segregated dormitories. That said, there was a great deal of pairing-off early in the season and a lot of interpersonal activity. The Jewish tennis pro and a Protestant waitress who were virtually living together were said to be a good match because neither group was thought to have strong religio-cultural inhibitions against fornication. Reflecting the geographic area around Gloucester, most of the non-Jewish young people on staff were Catholic, and it was, after all, 1956 – a time of relative innocence.

I had lost most of my excess weight the year following graduation from Cathedral. That was all I lost. Probably the youngest of the hotel staff, I was totally inexperienced and quite virginal. Which didn't stop Marie. An attractive and spirited older girl – she was entering her senior year at Regis College – who had earlier paired off with Havana Roy. Marie and Roy were considered among the hottest couples among the hotel staff. However, the heat went out of that romance when Roy discovered that Marie would not fully and completely succumb to his Latin charms. He dumped her for one of the few non-college young women on the staff. As soon as the manicurist moved in with Roy, Marie ricocheted to the baby-faced high school graduate.

Perhaps I thought of Phyllis.

I had much more leisure time at the Oceanside than I had working two jobs the previous summer in the city. In Magnolia, most of the college kids worked three meals in a split shift as waitstaff in the dining room. My driving job was tied to the beach day, roughly from 10 to 4. I also did errands for the owners and for the chef, including picking up the printed menus in the neighboring town of Manchester-by-the-Sea. When stopped for a driving infraction in that exclusive preserve, I was dismissed once the town's lone police officer saw the South Boston address. A Swede up here in Manchester-by-the-Sea, the cop said in a thick mock brogue. Ah, sure, and ye deserve points just for finding this place.

Before my first leave-taking of my family, my father warned me about unspecified strange people to stay away from. This admonition came to mind when I found myself at the beach club alone one sunny afternoon before it opened for the season. At least, I thought I was alone. Having changed into swim trunks, I was fixing a towel to lie in the sun when one of the older hotel-circuit men appeared out of nowhere.

Hey kid, you're new this year aren't you?

Yes, said I, getting face-down on the towel. Just got here ten days ago.

In a flash, the man was on his knees, straddled over my prone city-white form, with one huge palm pinning my left shoulder to the terry cloth. I got some special suntan lotion here, kid, gonna put it on your back.

Frozen at the situation, and at the size and apparent strength of the man's hands, I was struggling to get up, fumbling for a way to protest when, apparently in deference to foreplay, the man asked,

So, where're you from? as he uncapped a container of lotion.

South Boston.

Oh. From Southie, eh? Ever hear of Joe-Joe the Golden Gloves champ?

The instant the words "He's my Dad," came out of my mouth, the erstwhile masseur got up off his knees, dropped the lotion, saying, You can handle this on your own, before disappearing.

Officials of 1961 Golden Gloves Tournament. Joe-Joe is seated third from left, Joe Heirty is on the right of him, rep. W.M. Bulger is far right, seated.

The few times our paths crossed the rest of that season, the man averted his eyes and went in the opposite direction.

Even when we weren't getting along, my father was protecting me.

The only other cultural surprise was my scrap with one of the kitchen staff. I had made friends with Freddy, a Puerto Rican dishwasher, perhaps the only minority on staff that summer. I would try my Sister School Spanish on him, and he would practice his English. One evening early in the season I came out of the staff dining room after supper to see a burly kitchen laborer taunting Freddy, telling him to go back to his own country.

Ever the smarty-pants, I stepped in, telling the bully that Puerto Rico was a part of the United States, and Freddy was in fact born in Miami, as I blunted a punch meant for my friend. This must have infuriated our colleague, who with one swing took out most of two of my lower teeth. Once the following melee was over, and my friends had helped me stem my bloody and interfering mouth, the chef came out and told me that he had fired the "bad apple," but that I should probably watch myself, because he only lived about ten minutes away.

This episode necessitated an unexpected trip back to Boston and a visit to Dr. Kendrick, the dentist near Joe's Spa, who capped the teeth. An unexpected bonus from this incident was Joe-Joe's quiet pride that his son was finally beginning to act normal. Couldn't go into the Municipal Building Gym, but I sure showed that bad apple from Gloucester that Southie boys take no guff.

Didn't matter that that was not quite the scenario, but he felt good about it – and I guess, so did I.

Truth is that early in the season, I did do some reading from Phyllis's list, but as I got to know people and felt more comfortable, the party atmosphere caught hold.

The staff ate together in their own dining room. They also hung out there between shifts, especially on non-beach days. Various and sundry beer parlors in Gloucester, Essex, and Rowley became frequent destinations. One of the members of the clique to which I gravitated, was the part-time pianist in the Rose Room. Recent UMass graduate Anna Mae Robinson, was a local mini-celebrity known for her earthy renditions of oldies like "Hard-Hearted Hannah, the Vamp of Savannah." She had a crush on an egg farmer, introducing her companions to a whole new strata of the area as we travelled from one working-class North Shore dive to another .

It didn't take long for me to become disabused of previous notions of the intellectual prowess and curiosity of my middle-class, soon-to-be college peers. I also learned that not all day students were rich. The picture I had of college being filled with well-dressed kids driving fancy new sports cars was considerably expanded by meeting and working with youngsters who were serving food all summer to earn tuition. Phyllis had told me about this reality, but Magnolia internalized it.

Because my job was part of the concierge system, I spent a lot of time with the bellhops. Some of the older men were making a career of working the hotel industry. Florida in winter, New England, the Catskills, the Poconos in summer. Some were in couple relationships with women who worked in the hotel as hairdressers, cocktail waitresses, or dining room hostesses.

All had a view of the world very different from that which I left behind in the Old Colony. Just as I left the Oceanside with a very different view of college students.

Carol had accomplished her objective.

Nana, the sisters, Phyllis and Marie didn't do badly, either.

Chapter Seventeen

City Point residents Kathleen and Eleanor in hats, outside 1794Columbia Rd, 1958.

It was in the first semester of my sophomore year at Boston University that Joe-Joe, on one of his many walks to Castle Island, saw a “To Let” sign on a top floor. Since the availability of desirable flats was usually communicated by word-of-mouth, he didn’t get too excited, but checked it out anyway. Turned out to be an oversized seven-room flat at the top of a three-decker on the corner of Columbia Road and O Street.

Lace curtain heaven.

Seventy-five dollars a month, plus utilities. Only two rooms did not have ocean views: the room assigned to the older of my two sisters, Eleanor – Zita rationalized by saying that she was never home, anyway -- and the bathroom.

After thirteen years my family moved out of the Old Colony and returned to private rental housing. My sisters were still in high school. Eleanor stayed on at St. Augustine's, Kathleen transferred to Nazareth because it was closer to home and Zita was concerned that she would have difficulty riding the bus to school every day.

It cost the family roughly twice what we spent to live in the project, but we had more than twice the space. And much more. The light was dazzling, air was better – except for airplane traffic. No neighbors under the windows, no drunks urinating in the hallway. Joe-Joe could do his Castle Island walk quicker and have more time to meet up with cronies. Catching her breath after climbing two flights of stairs, Zita could sit in her living room and look at the ocean. She loved it and never stopped talking about the view. The bus stopped literally at our back door on O Street, outweighing the 10-15 minutes longer ride to her job in the Back Bay. For her it was a one-way trip, because Joe-Joe usually picked her up after work.

Now that we're moving up to St. Brigid's, I'm going to have to get a good hat, Zita said when we were getting ready to move out of the project. In her new City Point persona, my mother could no longer feel comfortable wearing her pre-Vatican II kerchief to mass as she had at St.Augustine's. At this point the War had been over for a dozen years, Zita had returned to her insurance company job, meaning that both parents were working full time. Their oldest child was a college sophomore –

an oddity in their circle – the middle a high school senior, and the youngest two years behind her.

Public housing had done its job to stabilize this family. For us, it was time for the next step. In addition to the deteriorating physical and social conditions at the Old Colony, the prompting nudge was notification from the project management that our lease would not be renewed because we were over-income under the new policies. It was time for a needier family to have our five-room flat. Time for another kid to have my bedroom, and – hopefully – do his or her homework looking out the window, looking down East Ninth Street, across Mercer Street, and through the keyhole-like archway at the end to the water. My new room had a direct view of the ocean over the rooftops of the yacht clubs across the street.

Life got better for everyone. Joe-Joe cut back on his benders, Zita was working on becoming a Grande Dame, Eleanor discovered City Point and made new friends, and she easily mastered riding the Bay View bus all dozen stops from O Street to St. Augustine's High. Kathleen fussed about it, but she made a good transition to Nazareth High School, walking the few blocks from her new home. I had made it through the freshman year at BU. Still dependent on rote learning techniques, I plodded through the first two semesters. But by the start of the sophomore year, I was beginning to internalize material and become exhilarated by the discovery of whole new worlds.

One of the many other features of our new location was proximity to Kelly's Landing, the seasonal fried food emporium on the Strandway down the street. Zita never went back to Dorgan's, but held her appetite for fried clams until Kelly's opened in the spring. That first May we were City Point residents, my Kim Novak look-alike sister Eleanor was approached by one of the sisters at St. Augustine's.

Eleanor, now you may know that every year the faculty is contacted by the Kelly family to see if we can recommend any of our outstanding young women to work at the Landing for the summer. And, I've been thinking about you. That's only a few blocks from where you're living now, is it not?

Yes, Sister.

And I know they like to have girls with personality. Certainly you qualify in that department.

Thank you, Sister.

But, there is something else, Eleanor.

And, what is that, Sister?

Well, your math grades indicate you could handle making change, certainly. But, there is one thing . . .

Oh?

Eleanor, when St. Augustine's High School recommends a girl, we have our reputation at stake here. We must be sure that any girl we send to the Kellys will represent us well. That means not only hard work is expected, but also a ladylike comportment. You can do it, Eleanor, I am confident that you can. Always remember, Eleanor, you're there to work, to make St. Augustine's proud of you. You're not there to meet boys.

Sister's admonition flew in the face of the experience of generations of Southie youngsters. The one central place for teenagers, more neutral than any street corner in town, was Kelly's Landing. Whether you were hungry or not, you appeared there at least once during a weekend, joining the throngs of people from all over the metropolitan area. They came to walk to Castle Island, to walk around Pleasure Bay, and to eat at Kelly's.

This was a time of Friday abstinence. Lines for fried clams and fish and chips began forming in the late afternoon, and usually didn't let up until around eight o'clock. The Kelly women on the counter occasionally got ruffled when the local police station would come in for an especially large order – always gratis -- in the midst of this Friday rush. But, that didn't dampen their enthusiasm for giving freebies. Most of the convents in town were the recipients of surprise deliveries of the treasured fried delicacies.

It was not just the location of Kelly's, right there on the ocean. For those who drove from Medford, Quincy, Brighton, Brookline and other regions of the Diaspora, it was also about the quality of the food.

A whole family of Gorham boys worked the kitchen for more than a generation. They did most of the fry work, and consequently were pursued by hordes of fried clam fans who wanted the recipe. Was it the batter? Were the clams a special kind? Maybe it's the oil? Guys bribed them with cases of beer, women threw themselves at them. But, with the steadfastness of the CIA, the secret never passed the Gorham boys' lips.

Years after the Landing closed, Frank Gorham, youngest of the crew, let it out.

There never was a secret recipe, Frank said. "The secret was that we used the best of everything – clams, flour, oil – and, here's the real hitch: we clean the oil frequently. There was so much volume that we changed it often, too. That made the food light and fresh.

Dickey Kelly, the family scion running the present iteration of Kelly's Landing on L Street at Emerson, agreed. My folks ran a quality place. They were serving food to their neighbors. They knew it had to be the best.

In the midst of all of this, Sister was on to something. Kelly's was a great place for teens to come together. Adjacent to the beach, and positioned on its own pier, opposite Farragut Park, it was a natural. The girls who worked the counter became mini celebrities for guys from all over to check out. Guys who worked as life guards next door were similarly ogled by girls who passed the word. After working a long, hot weekend shift, the workers from Kellys would often cool off in a midnight swim behind the shop.

Eleanor was in her element at Kelly's. She met a whole new circle of friends, and had boys literally following her home. But, best of all, one of her new co-workers was the most beautiful girl in all of South Boston. Mary Daigle was a vivacious green-eyed French girl from City Point, whose father owned the deep-sea fishing boats that ran from Kelly's Landing. He also had Frenchie's Barber Shop at P and Fifth where he cut hair when he was not on the boats or working at Domino Sugar. Naturally, Eleanor introduced Mary to her brother. Being no fool, I married her. Eventually. Which ended my fascination with older women: she was five years my junior.

But we get ahead of our story.

How things turned out

Kelly's Landing after 1956 hurricane.

Boston University in the 1950s was a kaleidoscope of stimulation. Howard Thurman – Martin Luther King, Jr.'s mentor -- was Dean of Chapel. The Hungarian Revolution sent scores of refugee students to BU. Young men back from Korea were choosing urban colleges to complete their education on the GI Bill. Affluent post-war families from outside commuting distance discovered Boston as a place to send their children to go to college. And, Boston University, while not to be confused with the Ivies, was close enough geographically.

After thirteen years with the good sisters, I had no idea how stimulating education could be. Sure, I was behind my cohorts in terms of preparation for college. I lacked exposure to the Classics, and was weak in sequential thinking and deductive reasoning. But, when it came to understanding the Middle Ages and the Renaissance, I had that religious material down pat.

After early graduation, I went to Naval Officers Candidate School and served as a naval journalist primarily in the Middle East. The wedding at St. Bridgid's followed by a reception at the Boston Yacht Club happened after I returned home and had secured an appropriately abysmally low-paying job in publishing. With my wife's support, my speech impediment subsided into controllability. After several years in Dorchester learning how to be community activists, we raised our three sons in Newton.

Finally figuring out how to do it, I went back to school to complete a master's degree in the early '80's and a doctorate in '88. In the midst of the national social upheaval in the late '60s, I had left a position as promotion director of Pilgrim Press, a Boston-based publisher to become a social worker in the inner city. Among my achievements are the foundation of a macro-level elder-service agency in Boston, Kit Clark Senior Services, and the leadership of a major Church-related charity -- Catholic Charities and Catholic Social Services -- in which role I had the opportunity to boss around sisters. However, to my knowledge, I never kept them from the circus.

Nana Delia died on the eve of St. Patrick's Day, 1964 at age 84. Just a year before, I was thrilled to have her meet her first great-grandchild, our eldest son Joel.

After a major heart attack, Joe-Joe radically curtailed his drinking and increased his involvement in community and political affairs, including a run at State Representative. However, he withdrew in favor of a newcomer named William M. Bulger. Later, at age 60, he suffered his second and fatal heart attack at the wake of a former State Secretary and gubernatorial candidate, Joe Ward. Father and son had reconciled years earlier.

Zita retired from American Mutual five years after Joe-Joe died, learned to drive after decades of back-seat nagging, and moved to Scituate to live with her daughter Eleanor who had been pried out of her Ticknor Street three-decker. Zita traveled with her sister Madeline and other girl friends. After twenty-two years a widow, she followed her husband at 83 years of age.

WARD 7 UNITE

DOOLIN IS RIGHT

for Representative

Joseph P.

DOOLIN

DEMOCRAT

Primaries: Tues., Sept. 13, 1960

23

Joe-Joe ran for office in 1960; pulled out to support newcomer William M. Bulger.

Lifelong South Boston resident

Married to the former Zita M. Pelose

Father of three children, Eleanor M., Kathleen A. and Joseph, Jr., who recently graduated cum laude from Boston University and is currently in Officers' Candidate School at the Naval Training Station in Newport, R. I.

EDUCATION:

Attended St. Augustine's Parochial School

South Boston High School

Wentworth Institute of Engineering

ORGANIZATIONS:

Director of South Boston Citizens' Association

Knights of Columbus

St. Brigid's Holy Name Society

Elected delegate to the 1960 State Convention from Ward 7

Member of Boston Democratic City Committee from Ward 7

OCCUPATION:

Construction Engineer

Joe Doolin with his past experience and working knowledge of the needs of the people of Ward 7 is well qualified to represent them.

Member of Local 804 AFL-CIO

RESIDENCE:

1794 Columbia Road, AN 4-3561

A VOTE FOR DOOLIN IS A VOTE FOR A BETTER WARD 7

Back of campaign card.

Carol wasn't so lucky. She was shot and murdered in Copley Square in late 1959. Thirty years of age. Police ascribed it to a lover's triangle among the woman, one of her boy friends who often invited me to dinner with the couple, and an amorous cab driver. I never bought it. But, that's another book. See *Death in Copley Square*.

Sister Anne Francesca apparently got away with her extracurricular lesson in sex education. She came out of the convent in the turmoil of the 1960's and its aftermath. A dozen years later, she died of cancer. On hearing this from a member of her family at one of the hotels they owned, it was like hearing that an immortal subject in a Giotto mural had died. The shock being not so much the shock of death, but the shock of coming to grips with her humanity. With one of Boston's most famous hotels as the backdrop, plus the distance of time and education, Saint Augustine's – and even Sister Anne Francesca -- seemed eons and continents away.

But not forgotten.

At that time, I worked closely with a great many sisters. Only a couple, however, still wore anything that could be mistaken for a habit. It occurred to me that as sad as I was to hear of the early death of Sister Ann Francesca, I was strangely relieved that I didn't know her in the post-Vatican II reality of women religious. There was clearly something about the carefully pressed habit, the starched wimple, the clack of the wooden rosaries around her waist, the smell of whatever it was that constituted the "convent smell" that added to her mystique for thirteen and fourteen-year-old boys. Seeing her in street clothes, even if she did look a lot like Ann Blythe, would not have done it.

Empty-nesters after nearly four decades of exile, my wife and I acquired a condo in South Boston early in the new millennium, while also spending very long summers on Cape Cod, close to several family members.

Not long after I returned to South Boston, I took a wrong turn and found myself in the midst of a housing project. Driving down my old street, two things struck me. Saplings of a half century ago were now full grown trees lining the harsh sidewalks, providing a surprising touch of grace and of softness. And cars, cars were everywhere. So were pickups, SUVs, and motorcycles. When my family moved in during the World War II years, there were no more than half a dozen automobiles on the entire street, spanning more than two blocks.

There was an open parking space around the corner from where I used to live. I parked, and walked toward the squat, institutional-looking red-brick building, identical to scores of others in the development. It was late afternoon of a school day; I wondered why there were so few kids in evidence. As I drew nearer, I noticed that everything was darker and grimier. Much. Only partly because where there was once grass and children's play equipment there were now expanses of black tar littered with evidences of a to-go society.

I found the window of the bedroom that was mine for so many years. Looking the other way, it was still there: The opening. As a child I used to look out my bedroom window at the building that ended the street, a block away. This building blocked the street from playing fields and the beach beyond, except for an archway cut through at street level providing pedestrian access. From the desk under my bedroom window I spent countless hours looking through that arch, where I could see open sky, and sometimes I thought, the sea beyond.

For me, that archway had always represented the gate to the world outside the project walls.

Author's study, Old Colony, 1955.

Although I hadn't lived here for well over forty years, for the past quarter century it was part of the geography in which I worked, and I was therefore fully aware that a strange guy hanging around this neighborhood could trigger questions. Across the street I found a bench in the deserted schoolyard, and sat, looking over at where I used to live.

The short rise of stairs to the front door was empty that afternoon. Mists of so many years could not block memories of the gatherings of parents and children on this stoop. Kids I played with. The chants of street games. Fun times as well as painful times. The stuff of life. I suddenly realized that this place was home. This was where I grew up. It was not until well after marriage that I lived in any place longer than I lived in the Old Colony.

Consciously or unconsciously, we are all the products of the lives that went before us. My grandparents' immigrant experience had as much impact on my young psyche as my parents' survival of the Great Depression. My father's clannishness and tribal loyalties were probably more than just the South Boston in the boy, but undoubtedly also a way to cope with a teenage boy's loss of his mother to mental illness and the resultant bonding with siblings closest in age. My mother's feelings of low self-worth were probably connected with her father's sense of being the Other as an Italian in Irish and Yankee Boston at the turn of the twentieth century.

They both did the best they could with what they had to deal with. My sisters and I are proud to have had them as parents. Just as we feel proud and privileged to have grown up in South Boston at mid-century.

Like computer pop-ups, some things jumped forward in front of others:

Coming down those stairs with a brand-new bike on my tenth birthday, my father behind me, holding up the rear wheel.

The sounds from my sisters' window of Zita spanking the two girls while she sang "Lady of Spain" to mask their howling.

My father stumbling up the stairs, holding the railing with both hands.

A fine rain had started. I stood up, readying to go to my car. Then the visitor to this strange but so familiar place thought he saw something that caused him to sit back down. There was a man in the distance, trotting toward the archway, holding onto the rear of a bicycle as a young boy pumped it unsteadily.

Tear or rain, I brushed my eyes as I got up from the hard metal bench and walked toward my car, not looking back at where I came from.

I didn’t have to.
I was home.

Mary Elizabeth Daigle Doolin , Nazareth High School, 1959.

ACKNOWLEDGEMENTS

Utmost thanks to my beloved wife Mary Elizabeth Daigle Doolin, M.Ed., who urged me to write this book. And, as another child of South Boston – however younger -- she has helped fill in the interstices of memory, and has served as Editor Confidante in Chief.

My dear sisters and first readers, Eleanor Margaret Doolin McLaughlin, RN, MBA; Kathleen Ann Doolin McLellan RN, who bear both the names and the spirit of our paternal aunts, Margaret and Anna.

The work of Dr.Thomas H. O'Connor, particularly *South Boston My Home Town* is reflected in some of that which you see here.

The good sisters of Notre Dame, who dutifully staffed St.Augustine's School, and the Sisters of Saint Joseph at Cathedral High School provided to me, and generations of city kids before and after, the best education of which they were capable.

My sons, Dr. Seth Doolin, who served as publisher for this edition, deserves accolades for his technical proficiency and patience; and Matthew Doolin, BA, served as chief artistic director, and has earned kudos for his vision and creative energy. Thank you, Seth and Matt.

Through the scrapbook of human memory, this book tells the story of one project family, and the thirteen years we spent in public housing. I try to share vignettes of this period – and prior family events that shaped it -- through the eyes of a boy growing up in this newly created mid-twentieth century urban village. My eyes. Like most families, ours had its share of successes and failures, heartbreaks and joy, squabbles and supports.

Perhaps because of those shared challenges, the remaining members of our family remain close and loving to this day.

This collection of stories is based on the author's memory. Names of neighbors and classmates have been changed to preserve privacy.

Joseph Doolin, Osterville, Massachusetts, September 4, 2011

Joseph Doolin is President Emeritus of Catholic Charities, and Secretary for Social Services, Archdiocese of Boston. Previously, he served as the founding Executive Director of Kit Clark Senior Services. He has written several scholarly articles on gerontology and homelessness, as well as a regular column in Boston's Catholic weekly, The Pilot.

Death in Copley Square is a sequel to *South Boston Boy*.

Illustrations

Photographs on pp. 12, 13, 61, 84, 187, 203, 210, and 223 are used courtesy of the Trustees of the Boston Public Library, Print Department.

Cover photograph, and those on pp. 32, 73, 82, 83, 120, 128, 130, 143, 152, 154, and 247 are used courtesy of Anthony Sammarco.

Image on p. 125 is from "The Phantom Empire" as found on image.google.com. as is image on p. 219.

Photographs on pp. 9 and 97 are courtesy of my cousin, George E. Butler.

All other photographs are from the Doolin family archives.

Special thanks to Kathleen P. Dunn of the Boston Public Library Print Department for the professional expertise that she has shared with me.

Made in the USA
Charleston, SC
03 November 2011